LETTERS FROM COLETTE

LETTERS FROM

Colette

SELECTED AND

TRANSLATED BY

ROBERT PHELPS

FARRAR STRAUS GIROUX

NEW YORK

Translation copyright © 1980 by Farrar, Straus and Giroux, Inc.
Introduction, compilation, and editing copyright © 1980 by Robert Phelps
Originally published in French in five separate volumes:
Lettres à Hélène Picard, Lettres à Marguerite Moreno,
Lettres de la vagabonde, Lettres au petit corsaire,
Lettres à ses pairs © 1958, 1959, 1961, 1963, 1973 by Flammarion
All rights reserved
Published simultaneously in Canada by McGraw-Hill Ryerson Ltd., Toronto
Printed in the United States of America
Designed by Cynthia Krupat
First edition, 1980
Library of Congress Cataloging in Publication Data
Colette, Sidonie Gabrielle, 1873–1954.
Letters from Colette.
1. Colette, Sidonie Gabrielle, 1873–1954—Correspondence.
2. Authors, French—20th century—Correspondence.
I. Phelps, Robert. II. Title.
PQ2605.O28Z53 1980 848'.91209 [B] 80-20680

EDITOR'S NOTE

A quarter of a century after her death in 1954, Colette continues to emerge not only as the widely admired author of *Chéri, Gigi*, and *La Vagabonde*, and as one of the subtlest stylists ever to explore the resources of the French language, but as a savory, even fierce personality in her own right. As her autobiographical *Earthly Paradise* made clear, Colette is her own most memorable character, a sort of twentieth-century earth goddess who lived most of her life in Paris, watching the world around her so attentively that she was able to describe how a single rose petal sounds when it falls. Now, as a further gloss to her life, we are beginning to have her letters.

According to Maurice Goudeket, her third husband, she averaged half a dozen daily, all spontaneous, abundant, dashed-off, like nothing so much as an armful of field flowers, fresh, fragrant, still sparkling with dew, which Ceres, let's say, brought in from her morning walk. Unlike certain other great writers—Thomas Mann, for instance, or Yeats or Rilke—who tend to be formal, posed, and even posturing, in their correspondence, Colette is everywhere impulsive and intimate. She writes about her daily ambience, about weather and her new apartment, about moral and physical health, about how to witch a well or pet a panther, about deadlines and earning a living, about roses and truffles and Beaujolais and brie and planting tangerine trees and learning (at fifty!) to ski. There is good gossip and intelligent malice and reticent tenderness on every page: and, above all, "*pas de littérature.*"

In France, as of 1980, five volumes of these bulletins have been published. The first three were devoted to single correspondents—actress Marguerite Moreno, poet Hélène Picard, and a younger writer, Renée Hamon, whom Colette nicknamed the "little pirate." The other two volumes included letters to assorted friends and associates in the theater and the arts. In addition, Maurice Goudeket has published excerpts from letters to himself in *La Douceur de vieillir* (*The Delights of Growing Old*), and bits from other correspondences—to Colette's stepson, Renaud de Jouvenel, for example—have appeared in periodicals and catalogues.

But the principal collections of letters are yet to come: to Colette's daughter, notably; to her three husbands, Willy, Henry de Jouvenel, and Maurice Goudeket; and to such important friends as the Marquise de Belbeuf, with whom she lived after her first marriage. A large number to Sido, Colette's mother, were destroyed in 1914, but other hefty packets—to novelist Germaine Beaumont, to violinist Hélène Jourdan-Morhange, to assorted members of the de Jouvenel family—are all waiting—not to mention half a century's communication with publishers and editors.

So the present selection, mostly taken from the five French volumes published by Flammarion and scrupulously edited by Claude Pichois and Roberte Forbin, can make no claim to being definitive. I have followed my own taste, trimming freely and trying simply to show Colette in her daily zest, meeting her deadlines, paying her bills, at play with her family and friends, at work in the theater, on the lecture platform, in her short-lived beauty salon, and at her lifelong writing desk. Letters and memoirs to come will certainly deepen the image this book makes, but it is unlikely that they will radically alter it.

Colette's life story is that of a robust country girl who comes to the big city and prevails, earning herself a place in the sun. Oddly enough, Colette always disclaimed any sense of literary vocation, insisting that she became a writer because she was paid to do so. ("I knew how to climb trees and how to whistle and run," she said, but no one paid her to do that.) So she wrote, "slowly, submissively, patiently," without any pretention and theory, and obliging herself only to remain as faithful as possible to what she had seen and felt. In a review of *As You Like It*, she once observed that "Shakespeare wrote without knowing that he would become Shakespeare." The same might be said of Colette.

Nor can any comparable writer be said to have flourished so independently of the tastes and ideologies of the time. Except for automobiles and electric lights, Colette's world is as uncontemporary as the seventeenth century. Her first book was published in 1900, when Paris was the epicenter of Europe. The opera of the year was *Tosca*. Bernhardt was playing in *L'Aiglon*. Freud published *The Interpretation of Dreams*, and Oscar Wilde had taken refuge on the Left Bank. It was the year of the Boxer Rebellion, the Boer War, and the Zeppelin.

The next half century, along with some fifty more books by Colette, saw the rise of mighty movements and milestones in the arts: Picasso, Joyce, Stravinsky, Eliot, Gide, and that gallant thrust called Modernism, not to mention Surrealism, Dadaism, Cubism,

Neo-Romanticism, Marxism, etc. At no point in her life did Colette join or relate to any of this group play. She wrote a libretto for Ravel, but it had nothing to do with Modern Music. Her second husband was a distinguished diplomat and one of her stepsons an important economist, but she herself remained as apolitical as the strawberries she raised on the balcony of her Claridge Hotel room. And though today, for many of her readers, Colette is the embodiment of the emancipated woman, whose social status and economy and sex life are unhectored by male hegemony, she never thought of herself as representing anything. Her only "role" amounted to creating, or becoming, the self we call Colette.

There is a line from Shakespeare's *All's Well That Ends Well* that kept humming in my mind all through the summer by the sea that I worked on this translation:

> *... simply the thing I am*
> *Shall make me live.*

In her least postcard, as well as in her novels, her gardens, her friendships, and her loves, it seems to me that Colette's lifetime, and lifework, fulfills this promise.

Robert Phelps

Gayhead, Mass.
July 1979

I must (again) thank Madame Colette de Jouvenel for the privilege of spending several months in her mother's company, and at the same time express my gratitude to Claude Pichois and Roberte Forbin for the use of their meticulous *texte établi et annoté* in the Flammarion editions of Colette's letters.

R.P.

CHRONOLOGY

1829 Colette's father, Jules-Joseph Colette (Le Capitaine), born in Toulon.

1835 Colette's mother, Adèle-Eugénie-Sidonie Colette (Sido), born in Paris.

1873 January 28, at 10:00 p.m.: Sidonie-Gabrielle Colette born in Saint-Sauveur-en-Puisaye, Yonne, France.

1890 Public sale of the Colette family's goods and home. Colette and her parents move to Chatillon-Coligny, Loiret.

1893 Marriage of Colette to Henri Gauthiers-Villars, known as Willy. The newlyweds settle on the Left Bank in Paris, at 28, rue Jacob. Colette enters the literary and artistic world, coming to know and be known by Proust, Pierre Louÿs, Jules Renard, Ravel, Debussy, Fauré, etc.

1900 Publication of *Claudine à l'école*, the first of an enormously successful quartet of books about a young country girl who comes to Paris. Though written by Colette, they appeared under Willy's name only.

1904 *Dialogues de bêtes*, a series of conversation pieces featuring an angora cat and a bulldog: signed Colette Willy.

1905 September 17: death of Le Capitaine.

1906 Separation from Willy, and alliance with the Marquise de Belbeuf (Missy). Debut as a mime dancer.

1907 Colette appears at the Moulin Rouge in a mime which features a passionate kiss between herself and Missy dressed as a man. A scandal ensues and the show is closed by the police.

1908 *Les Vrilles de la vigne*, autobiographical sketches and short stories.

1910 While continuing to appear on stage, Colette publishes *La Vagabonde*. On June 21, her divorce from Willy is made final.

1911 Breaks with Missy, and takes a house at 57, rue Cortambert with Henry de Jouvenel, editor of *Le Matin*, a leading Paris daily.

1912 September 25: death of Sido, and destruction of Colette's letters to her.

December 19: marriage to Henry de Jouvenel.

1913 July 3: birth in Paris of Colette's daughter, Bel-Gazou, interrupting the serial publication of *L'Entrave*, the sequel to *La Vagabonde*.

1914 August: with the outbreak of war, Henry de Jouvenel is mobilized.

1915 Colette in Rome and Venice as a special reporter.

1916 *La Paix chez les bêtes*, an album of animal portraits.

1917 Colette again in Rome, writing film scripts.

1918 *Les Heures longues*, sketches about life on the home front, and *Dans la foule*, essays on public events.

1919 *Mitsou*, a short novel which made Proust weep. Colette takes over the literary page of *Le Matin*, and with the end of the war, resumes her Brittany summers in the house Missy gave her. The household includes not only Bel-Gazou and Henry's two sons, Bertrand and Renaud, but various associates on *Le Matin*.

1920 *Chéri*. Colette is named Chevalier de la Légion d'Honneur.

1921 *Chéri* dramatized.

1922 *La Maison de Claudine*: short stories about Colette's childhood in Burgundy.

1923 *Le Blé en herbe*: Colette's version of the Daphnis and Chloë story. December: separation from Henry de Jouvenel.

1924 *La Femme cachée*: twenty-two short stories.

1925 Colette tours as Léa in her adaptation of *Chéri*. Over the Easter holidays she meets Maurice Goudeket, who is to become her "best friend" and third husband.
December: première of *L'Enfant et les sortilèges*, Ravel's opera based on Colette's libretto.

1926 *La Fin de Chéri*. Colette buys a house, La Treille Muscate, in Saint-Tropez. Tours the South of France, playing the title role in her stage adaptation of *La Vagabonde*.

1927 Moves into an apartment in the Palais-Royal.

1928 *La Naissance du jour*.

1929 *La Seconde*. Travels in Spain and North Africa. Lectures in Berlin.

1930 *Sido*. July cruise along the Norwegian coast on the Rothschild yacht *Eros*.

1931 January 12: death of Willy. Colette moves to the top floor of the Claridge Hotel at 74, Avenue des Champs-Elysées.

1932 *Ces Plaisirs . . .* (later retitled *Le Pur et l'impur*). *Prisons et paradis*: portraits of animals, the good life in Saint-Tropez, and such celebrated friends as Chanel and Mistinguett.

1933 *La Chatte*. Begins a five-year stint as drama critic for *Le Journal*.

1934 *Duo*. Dialogue for Marc Allégret's film *Lac aux dames*.

1935 April 3: married to Maurice Goudeket.
June: visits New York on the maiden voyage of the *Normandie*.
October 5: death of Henry de Jouvenel.

1936 April 4: received into the Académie Royale de Langue et Littérature Françaises de Belgique.
Mes Apprentissages.

1937 *Bella-Vista*.

1938 Moves back to the Palais-Royal, settling in a sunny apartment at 9, rue de Beaujolais, where she remains for the rest of her life.

1939 *Le Toutounier*.
September 3: war with Germany. Colette makes overseas broadcasts to America.

1940 *Chambre d'hôtel*.
June 12: Colette leaves Paris for her daughter's house in Corrèze, returning to the Nazi-occupied capital in early September.

1941 Colette writes a weekly column about daily life and survival in Paris. *Julie de Carneilhan*. *Journal à rebours*.
December 12: Maurice Goudeket arrested by the Nazis and detained at a concentration camp in Compiègne.

1942 February 6: Goudeket liberated.
April–June: Colette treated with X-rays for sciatica.

October: *Gigi*, perhaps Colette's most famous story, is first published in *Présent*, a Lyons weekly.

1943 *Le Képi.*

October 16: death of Renée Hamon.

1944 June 29: suicide of Missy.

August 24: liberation of Paris.

Paris de ma fenêtre.

1945 February 1: death of Hélène Picard.

May 2: elected unanimously to the Académie Goncourt.

August 15: end of World War II.

1946 *L'Etoile vesper.*

March–April: to Geneva for arthritis cure.

1948 *Pour un herbier.*

July 14: death of Marguerite Moreno.

1949 *Le Fanal bleu.*

First of fifteen volumes of the *Oeuvres Complètes.*

1950 *En Pays connu.* Begins to spend winters in Monte Carlo.

1951–54 Final years, bedridden and in constant pain, but still writing—"*C'est mon métier!*"—and immensely famous, her windows overlooking the garden of the Palais-Royal having become a Parisian landmark.

August 3, 1954: dies. State funeral and burial in Père-Lachaise Cemetery. "Death does not interest me—not even my own."

LETTERS FROM COLETTE

Lucien Muhlfeld*

Paris, early January 1902

... *Claudine à Paris* is due to open later this month,† and I conjure you, Muhlfeld, to tear it apart favorably. It has nothing to do with either art or literature, of course. It's idiotic, and you should say so. But please also say that it will be a "box-office hit." It has to be, because we need the money. (This involuntary iambic shows you how exhausted I am ...)

Jeanne Muhlfeld

Paris, early 1902

Thanks to fatigue, I was in such a state of moral liquification yesterday evening that I did not tell you what I wanted to. Although Willy was dog-tired, he worked late after we came home, and after he'd gone out this morning, I had a chance to see what he's done to the manuscript of *Claudine en ménage*.

Having seriously broken up with Georgie (this is a fact), that spiteful boy is now determined to alter the character of Claudine's girlfriend Rézi to resemble Georgie. With a few

---

* Lucien Muhlfeld (1870–1902), distinguished novelist and drama critic for the powerful *L'Écho de Paris*. His wife, Jeanne, presided over a literary salon whose stars included Cocteau, Gide, Proust, and Valéry.
† Adapted by Willy and the actor Lugné-Poë from the first two Claudine books, *Claudine à Paris* opened January 21, 1902, with Polaire in the leading role. It was frequently revived in the following decade, notably in 1908, when Colette added autobiographical details and played the lead herself.

crude retouches here and there, he is succeeding. It's too brutal, but there she is—or there she would be—frightfully recognizable. This must not be allowed to happen. It's a trick unworthy of Willy, or almost anyone. As you can see, I am worried—above all for Willy, since after all I have my own reasons for being less concerned about . . . Georgie.*

My dear friend, you know that it would only take a word from you or from Lucien, or from the two of you, to discourage Willy from doing this. Tell him I have approached you. You will be doing him a real service. But hurry . . .

Paris, early June 1902

. . . My bulldogs are adorable, with faces like toads that have been sat on. Madame Mardrus,† whom I do not know in the least, flings her new collection of poems, *Ferveur*, in my face. *Claudine à Paris* will finish its unhoped-for if not glorious career at the Bouffes-Parisiens Theater with a total of 130 performances. But . . . all of that is not worth the color of the sky at 5 a.m. at Monts-Boucons,‡ or the poignant pillage of a nest of garter snakes in the meadow, with the very young serpents looking like so many silk shoelaces. Oh, Muhlfeld! kiss the beetle which offers you its forehead. *Claudine en ménage* salutes you, with the news that it has 70,000 copies in print this week . . .

---

* Georgie was Willy's otherwise unidentified mistress, upon whose personality he was vengefully attempting to model a character in *Claudine en ménage*. Whether or not Colette and the Muhlfelds persuaded him to remove his "crude retouches" cannot be determined. *Claudine en ménage* was published in May 1902.

† Lucie Delarue-Mardrus (1880–1945), wife of the French translator of the *Arabian Nights*. A prolific novelist and poet, she was also a prominent member of the Parisian sapphic literary underground in the early twentieth century. There is a brief but winning portrait of her in *L'Étoile vesper*.

‡ A country house in Franche-Comté which Willy bought for Colette in 1902 and later sold. Its black-tiled roof and Directoire façade appear in *La Retraite sentimentale* as Casamène and in *Mes Apprentissages* under its own name.

Monts-Boucons, mid-July 1902

Do you recognize me, Jeanne? I'm wearing an apron with pockets, a broad-brimmed pink calico hat, little hobnailed boots, no rice powder, buckskin gloves holding large pruning scissors—and the heart of a girl. You cannot imagine the pure—and purgative—joy of eating black cherries which the sun has ripened on the tree. It rains, it shines, I get up at six and am in bed by nine. I am turning the color of a pig-skin valise. My account book is like a well-kept flower bed. It's my annual virtue debauch, almost clandestine, which debases me to the moral level of a day laborer . . . And now I must spray two apple trees which are prone to aphids . . . I can't tell you about the silver dawns and the apricot sunsets today because my mouth is full and I have made a bet with myself to eat four hundred nuts between lunch and dinner. Oh! that's not a record, of course, but when one must gather as well as shell the nuts . . .

*Marguerite Moreno**

Monts-Boucons, 1902

. . . Lots of wind here, with fan-shaped clouds, three dogs (one terrible), and hidden in a circle of trees, a trapeze, complete with parallel bars, poles, and ladders. I venture the timid workouts of a lady who fears breaking something on the one hand and being beaten by her husband on the other. I particularly admire myself doing a reverse somersault on the trapeze rings. In two lessons Toby-Chien has learned to climb the ladder. I'm reserving this surefire success against a time when I'm hard up.

---

* Marguerite Moreno (1871–1948) was, according to Maurice Goudeket, "Colette's greatest friend." Early in her career as an actress, she was associated with the Comédie Française. Later she had a successful two decades in films. She met Colette about 1894, a few years before she married Marcel Schwob, a minor man-of-letters who translated Ibsen and Dickens, and who was himself devoted to Colette.

The thought of having to leave soon makes me very sad. There is a divine odor of mushrooms everywhere. And then the perfume of the ripening apples evokes other years so powerfully . . .

Francis Jammes*

Paris, early May 1904

Sir, I am sending you two of your own books, with the request that you inscribe them with your name. They are worn with moving from Paris to the country and back all these years. But I intend to have them more solidly bound. Please be careful not to lose the yellow cover to *Clara d'Éllebeuse*. I never lend these books . . .

For the rest of my life, I shall patiently languish until Willy is rich enough to live elsewhere than in Paris, on a little hilltop which is my own . . . Kiki-la-Doucette died last year. Toby-Chien is a very tender puppy who will die of excessive feeling. That's my household. Please return the two books. I have all your others as well. Put anemones between the pages, and excuse me for addressing you so intimately. Willy admires you too, but less blindly, more modestly than I. Adieu, monsieur. I don't know how to finish my letter.

Comtesse Anna de Noailles†

Paris, July 1904

I have read *Le Visage émerveillé* and I am still overwhelmed by that sadness masterpieces inspire. But there is something

---

* Francis Jammes (1868–1938), poet and short-story writer who preached a simplistic but heartfelt call to nature. His writings are full of precise descriptions of animals, flowers, and non-urban life which appealed to Colette. He wrote a preface for the second edition of *Dialogues de bêtes* and a mutually admiring correspondence ensued.
† The Comtesse Anna de Noailles (1876–1933), a poet celebrated for her melancholy love poems (*Le Coeur innombrable*) and her vehement

else, harder to express, and which a sort of modesty inhibits. It seems to me that your books are so close to yourself, and one does not say to someone one does not know, "My God, how beautiful you are!"

I know perfectly well that when I reread your text a little more coldly, I shall be trying to determine "how it's done." But in your case I suspect that all I shall know is that when you write about the morning, or pain, or love, or light, or *la volupté*, I am convinced that no one has ever before written about *volupté*, or light or morning . . .

I remain, madame, with admiration, your Colette Willy.

Francis Jammes

Paris, mid-October 1904

. . . Our friend Vallette wants to publish the complete set of seven *Dialogues de bêtes*, and I should be gratified if you consented to write a little preface. It is neither nice nor gay to earn money with what one loves, but we live almost entirely that way. So could you let me know at once, so I may say yes or no to Vallette?

Paris, October 19, 1904

Ah! Monsieur, how I do love you! There has never been anything like your preface, and I would like to publish it by itself, without my own text tagging along behind it! This *Rehabilitation of Colette Willy* will be the beginning and the end of my literary pride, which will never exceed the ambition to be your friend.

And thanks to you Willy, who woke up grouchy, is feeling expansive for the rest of the day . . . and all because of the tender alacrity with which you have borne witness for his "girl."

---

volubility at the dinner table. Cocteau has left a vivid image of her in *Portraits-souvenir*. In 1934, Colette was elected to her seat in the Belgian Academy.

Paris, April 1906

. . . I have received both *L'Église habillée de feuilles* and *Pensée des jardins*. And I have not written you because I have been working in the theater and that, I suspect, will forever lower me in your esteem. But I know how to keep my place. The fact that I have played a faun at the Mathurin Theater and a young ninny at the Théâtre-Royal makes me arrogant with some people but humble with you. If you wish, I shall send you a photograph of me as a faun . . .

I cannot say anything about *L'Église habillée de feuilles* because I know nothing about God, and doubt if I shall ever understand much more. But the *Pensée* book is certainly you, it's the Francis Jammes I love. The day before yesterday I found on the fortifications a beautiful striped cat whom some abominable pig had abandoned in the cold with three kittens. I took all four up in my skirt and brought them home. And now they are secure. But my God, what desperate gratitude that cat expressed! Before such looks, one blushes, one says, "That's too much, I don't deserve that . . ."

Georges Wague*

Paris, September 8, 1906

Would you be free these days to come by at 4 p.m. to give pantomime lessons to the Marquise?† She wants to play

* Georges Wague, or Waag (1875–1960), made his pantomime debut in 1898 and was engaged to give lessons to Colette and the Marquise de Belbeuf in 1906. From then until 1912, he and Colette, together with his wife, Christiane Mendelys, toured extensively in such mimes as *La Chair* and *L'Oiseau de nuit*. In *La Vagabonde* he appears as Brague; in 1916 Colette was able to secure him a teaching position at the Conservatoire Nationale des Arts et Métiers.

† The Marquise de Belbeuf (1863–1944), known as "Missy," was the niece of Napoleon III. Divorced soon after her marriage, she habitually wore men's clothes ("since in women's clothes she looked like a transvestite," said Maurice Goudeket) and kept a lathe in her apartment. In the post-Willy years, she and Colette were very close, and their relationship lapsed only on the appearance of Henry de Jouvenel in 1911. In *Le Pur et l'impur*, she is portrayed as La Chevalière, whose "right, even whose duty, is never to be quite happy . . ."

the role of Franck. Be good enough to let me know your terms at the same time.

Paris, October 1907

I won't be coming to rehearsal this morning. I'm sorry to let you know so late, and there'll be no time to warn poor Chantrier. But it's midnight and I have a bad sore throat. I hope it won't turn out to be grippe. In any case, we'll have to make some other arrangement for our rehearsals. You wouldn't be able to do anything useful with me this morning, and besides I can't continue rehearsals with the morning cleaning going on, and bicycles circling around us and aerialists overhead. If Chantrier can give us a room with a piano we can rehearse in the afternoon or the evening . . .

Charles and Lucie Saglio*

Paris, winter 1907

I'm very put out! When I'm not to be found at 44, rue de Villejust, you come to 2, rue Georges-Ville. Any child knows that. At the office of *La Vie Parisienne*, the sardonic receptionist told me you had left, simply to annoy me. I was delivering an article, which I brought back with me and which I'll send by mail tomorrow. From now on, I'll buy my grilled chestnuts at another corner!

Pierre Louÿs†

Le Crotoy, summer 1908

You are right, one hundred times right, to forbid *Bilitis* going on the stage. Besides, I have dreamed of a younger Bilittis, rather than Bilittis herself (are there two *t*'s or one?), but it would be too much to dare to use the same

---

* Charles Saglio (1873–1950), the editor of *La Vie Parisienne*, a smart weekly in which Colette published dozens of her early stories, as well as *La Vagabonde*, *L'Entrave*, and *Chéri*.

† Pierre Louÿs (1870–1925), novelist and author of *Chansons de Bilitis*, a book of love lyrics presumably translated by Louÿs from a contemporary of Sappho, but actually written by himself. They were widely read at the

charming name. But if you, oh Pierre Louÿs, if you yourself were to find the leisure to write the little playlet, the beautiful Greek dialogue, which you once almost promised me, in Natalie's garden . . . Michel Mortier is going to open his new theater and he asks me to do something (as well he might, considering the unhoped-for box-office receipts I brought in at the Capucines Theater in Nice). I would be so happy . . . But I'm boring you. All the same, think about it, won't you?

Georges Wague

Le Crotoy, summer 1908

I had your letter this morning. I should like very much not to cause you to miss any performances of *La Chair*, which would be good for both of us, but I don't know if this will be possible, owing to the dates. Can you let me have them again? And can you assure me first-class traveling accommodations? I won't write any further, as I've been poisoned by some bad mussels. Nothing so tiresome in the world. For twenty-four hours I've been more knocked out than by a week's illness. Tomorrow will be better, I hope.

Lots of fish, and above all what shrimp, my dear! And a tempest of wind that has not let up for eight days. What's going on at the Apollo? I know they wanted Meg for their revue but she preferred to sign with *Parisiana* for the same price because the theater is smaller and better for her voice . . . I'm dickering with Brussels for very good terms, the same that Polaire gets, for fifteen performances beginning November 10. I'll be happy to see Chantrier and interested to hear him talk about his *Judith* project. With a good show, after our success with *La Chair*, we should be able to secure a two-month engagement somewhere.

---

turn of the century, and three were set to music by Debussy. Their elegantly precise narcissism had a substantial influence on Colette's own early prose (*Les Vrilles de la vigne*).

Amiens, fall 1908

But, Wague, you are extraordinary: do you really imagine that it is only to bungle your affairs that I am staying on in Paris until the 26th? If it were only a matter of the lecture at the Femina I could perhaps accommodate you (though the lecture itself is paying me fifteen louis). But, unhappily for me, I have other problems than the Femina appearance and *La Chair*, and I have to deal with them. If you had been able to contract for the 28th, 29th, 30th, it would fit my schedule. And you don't even tell me which theater in Lyons. Is it at the Eldorado? If so, I can write to Rasimi, the director. When I did *Claudine* for him, the receipts were good enough to make him accommodating now, I assure you. But you seem to think I am being deliberately difficult. After all, I kept a "polite" silence when you sent *La Chair* off to America with someone else playing my role, even though I was very disposed to go myself. In other words, you turned what might have been a very-nice-possibility into something-not-very-interesting. It is true that I am less available than Meg Villars. And I hope to become less and less so. But don't take this in bad part. I love to play in *La Chair* and I am eager to do so whenever I am free. Therefore, if you can arrange these three days in Lyons, do so, instead of quarreling with me. But do, please, tell me which theater!

Le Crotoy, September 1, 1908

. . . I had your card on returning from Geneva, where (and I say this with a charming modesty) I have just had a topping success. I hardly expected so much, as it has been a long time since Willy and I were notorious in Switzerland. The Protestant newspapers observed an admonishing silence, but I ignored them. The mere public was a love! They say the Genevans are cold and formal. Lord! And into the bargain, my box-office receipts were the largest in my career, and that is always a pleasure.

LETTERS FROM COLETTE ❦ 12

... All I ask this winter is to work. I have something in view for both of us—I'll tell you about it. I'll also send you the little ad that was used in newspapers and programs. Swiss advertising methods are a marvel, let me assure you! We'll be back in Paris on the 15th, when we're moving. I'm writing you this in the middle of a storm such as hasn't been seen here in thirty years. The house trembles, you can't open a door, and just now a huge shutter has been carried off like a scrap of paper ...

Le Crotoy, early September 1908
... I am urged, on several sides, to accept acting engagements—in a resident company as well as on tour—but I am not fool enough to abandon pantomime, *which I love*. Because—and this is curious—in a play in which I have had success—I have found myself suddenly seized with a need to stop speaking, and to express myself with gestures, body movement, dance rhythms instead. Silly, isn't it?

Brussels, November 14, 1908
I'm dog-tired. Today we had dress rehearsal for five and a half hours straight . . . The company is good, the staging coquettish, it's raining, and I'm covered with dust up to my nostrils. Willy appeared for a rehearsal and left a little after midnight. Good publicity. Little handbills with pictures of the cast passed out in the street. Bady is here, she amuses herself imitating Colette imitating Bady . . .

Léon Hamel*

Lyons, December 10, 1908
... I have an hour to myself before dinner and the opening, which is more leisure than I've had since arriving. The

---

* Léon Hamel (1858–1917), the model for Hamond in *La Vagabonde*, was a privately wealthy dilettante who met Colette in 1906 and remained an intimate friend until his death. Tender and tactful, he carried delicacy to the point of destroying the originals of all of Colette's letters, but only after copying their contents, with coded names, into the sort of schoolgirl's notebook Colette herself used.

people in Baret companies are used to touring and having
to change the show every four days. They rehearse morning,
noon, and night without batting an eyebrow. It's a good
school but a rough one. After tonight's performance, I can
rest up, but tomorrow morning the rest of the company begins rehearsing the show which will follow me. And they do
that for six months at a time! I really admire them. Interesting detail: the prompter disappeared this morning. He had
drunk too much and presumably gone somewhere to sleep
it off. Since I know my lines, it didn't bother me; but everyone was left dangling.

You were very kind to come with me to the station. All I
can tell you is that I am happy to have you as a friend.

Charles Saglio
Lyons, December 12, 1908

I'm coming back the 17th. May I see you Friday at the *Vie*
offices? Let me have a word at the rue Torricelli address.
Great success in every way except . . . I'm insufficiently paid.
You aren't forgetting me, I hope? Because I still need . . .
what you promised me. I'm bored here and pawing the
ground with impatience to get home. Lyons is dark and it
rains constantly. I'm nervous and disagreeable, though not
to you.

Lucien Solvay*
Brussels, February 1909

In the days when Willy did me the dubious honor of signing
my novels, he would occasionally insert into my texts a few
words designed to gratify his personal spite. He used to call
this collaborating. In *Minne*, this "collaboration" consisted
in giving to certain characters the names of esteemed
confreres, notably yours. In resuming ownership of *Minne*
and *Les Égarements de Minne*, and refashioning them into

---

* Lucien Solvay (1851–1950), poet, novelist, and critic, was the original
of Sidney in *L'Ingénue libertine*.

a single volume called *L'Ingénue libertine*, my first concern has been to get rid of this impropriety. I am sending you a copy with my thanks and confraternal sympathy.

Léon Hamel

Paris, February 28, 1909

Tomorrow I play at the Comédie Royale for the last time, and I won't be sorry. We're doing our best to defend ourselves against the grippe. Missy has a wretched cold, and then this muddy snow, this slimy chill. Atrocious. Where you are, the snow must at least be cleaner.

I've had some very ugly news in the past few days . . . and naturally it originated with Willy.

Briefly, he has sold, without my knowing it, *all* the rights to the *Claudines* to their publishers for next to nothing, and thus these books which so entirely belong to me (morally speaking) are now lost to us both forever. Given the conditions of the sale, one would say that he truly wished not only to make very little but to assure himself that even after his death I would never regain possession of these books, which are mine. It was a deep shock to realize this, and I wrote him accordingly. He replied to my cry of despair with a cold, almost menacing letter, and I think that after the necessary explanation which will take place when he is back from Monte Carlo day after tomorrow, it will all be over between us.

Just think that, after three years of separation, I am still (and too often) discovering further betrayals about which I knew nothing. But I'm letting myself be carried away by my "tale of woes." Excuse me. We continue to have dinner chez Palmyre, who spoils us with motherly attentions, makes us presents, gives us fresh fruits, broils little beefsteaks for Missy, and yesterday we had to see the three little newborn bulldogs that her bitch Bellotte has just produced. Palmyre's maternal pride knew no bounds. She was delirious. I'm sure she would feel less passion for her own child.

Did you know that we went to the Wagram Ball as Pierrots? We accompanied Édouard de Max and Véra Sergine, who were neither masked nor costumed. Sergine conducted her pale, serious face through the festivities with an air of profound boredom, and afterwards we went on to supper chez Palmyre.

There we learned—by way of J. de Bellune—that at the dance in Nice the Baroness Van Zuylen appeared in her box in a tuxedo and with mustaches! She was accompanied by the Baroness Ricoy, also in a tuxedo, and looking emaciated beside her elephantine friend. They were recognized and hectored, but the Baroness Van Zuylen replied with a string of very masculine oaths.

What do you think of the new fountain pen I'm writing with? It's a gift from Missy, along with some intoxicating notebooks, with ruled, detachable pages—but I'll show them to you when you're here. In the next issue of *Akadémos*, you will find some butterflies from the Forêt de Crécy . . .

Georges Wague
Toulouse, April 29, 1909
. . . If the Alhambra cannot pay me as much as the Gaîté-Rochechouart, so much for the Alhambra. It's an outfit which should be able to pay, at the least, *reasonably*. And then, too, when I have a name with proved box-office value, why should I contract myself never to get more than five louis? When *shall* I raise my price? When I'm as old as Otéro? If business is poor, so much for business. Two hundred francs outside Paris, one-fifty in Paris . . .

Léon Hamel
Le Crotoy, September 2, 1909
For three days we've been having superb tides, which come right up to the house . . . and today the weather is deliciously alarming, with the sea striped with the most caressing blues and greens. We're going off to Berck by automobile.

And oh yes, there is some news: the day before yesterday I began what will, I hope, be a sort of novel . . . I am not beginning without apprehension, I admit, and this makes me peevish and nervous. But Missy is in good shape and we expect to leave for Brittany in a few days, to visit the villas. If the weather is good it will be a delicious trip . . .

André Rouveyre*

Paris, December 1, 1909

Above all, please notice that I did not dare carry off the red chalk drawing you gave me in your studio . . . I am bold in every respect, except at being a sponger.

Now: listen: Saturday, I am "reading" something at Sacha Guitry's afternoon at the Gymnase. I must be there by four o'clock, which would give us only two hours for you to draw and myself to purr. Sunday, I have matinee and evening performances. Monday is impossible. But I have another idea. Come, either Saturday or Sunday, before dinner, at seven or seven-thirty. Stay for dinner and until ten o'clock (when I have to leave for the theater). We'll chatter and you can draw. Then we'll make a proper appointment for a less hectic afternoon. This is simplest, I think. But answer at once, so I'll know which day. And if La Gandara wants to come, fine. He will excuse me, I hope, for inviting him so cavalierly?

Charles Saglio

Paris, February 22, 1910

This is not to tease you, or to confess any lack of self-confidence. It's simply that I have just reread what I have done up to now with *La Vagabonde*, and I realize what is missing and what I must change. Therefore, I ask you to

* André Rouveyre (1879–1962) was notorious as a caricaturist. He studied with Gustave Moreau at the same time as Matisse and was the friend of Apollinaire and Paul Léautaud.

postpone its appearance in *La Vie* until May 15. I want to give you a finished manuscript, worthy of you as well as myself. Write to me at the Hôtel Moderne, Grenoble. I'm leaving today.

André Rouveyre

Paris, June 23, 1910

Dear Rouveyre, do excuse me. I had just enough time to eat your strawberries, wipe my mouth, and leave for Saint-Malo . . . You were very kind to think of the glutton that I am and I thank you. Missy, who lives above this world and nourishes herself on Havana smoke, thanks you too, but she doesn't dare touch strawberries—they give her hives. At Saint-Malo, the sea was flattened with the heat. Oh, Rouveyre, when we are able to live in that corner which is now our own, you will come to see it and you'll tell me if it isn't truly the most beautiful in the world.

I am now divorced, you know.

Léon Hamel

Dijon, September 22, 1910

. . . The opening, last night, was epic. The orchestra conductor, as we saw too late, was not an orchestra conductor but a wine merchant. Musically, the evening was a disaster, for the other numbers as well as our own. Backstage everyone was howling, and the audience booed the conductor. It was stunning! Wague called him an assassin, and Christine Kerf called him an ass. We've been rehearsing all day today, and thanks to the orchestra players, who are good, I hope tonight will be better.

I have a little cat on my knees, lost, weak, and only needing to be fed. He's terribly frail at the moment. If I don't find someone to adopt him, I'll take him with me. He'll be my traveling companion. A hotel room is always improved by the presence of an animal.

Charles Saglio

Paris, early October 1910

Here I am. I'm back from Dijon, by way of Marseilles, but I leave again for Biarritz on Sunday. Conclusion: substantial sums are necessary. One thousand francs, isn't it? May I find you Friday between 5:30 and 6:00 at the *Vie* office *without fail*? A *pneumatique*, please, or a telephone call (521.92) to your ex-Vagabonde.

Léon Hamel

Naples, November 12, 1910

. . . I've barely arrived in a blue and gold heat which, in spite of myself, enchants me. The trip was long—two nights in a Pullman—which isn't restful. But the weather is lovely here and the Bay of Naples has produced on me what Wague calls a "marked effect."

Naples, November 15, 1910

. . . I'll never manage to write you a letter. Today—boat, car, boat again, storm, uncomfortable but amusing disembarkment. At the moment, a real tempest. Impossible to open a window . . .

Naples, November 19, 1910

I doubt if I'll be able to write the letter you ask for until I am back in Paris. It sounds idiotic, but here I am too close to what I am seeing, and above all, I want to see too much in too little time. I am too much the Cook's tourist. In spite of a storm, we have been to see Herculaneum today. But I remained cold before so much marble. And what is this sinister cave to me, with its perspiring walls that could hold ten thousand spectators and its actors' dressing rooms as poorly arranged as they are today? I'll take the Temple of Nero, or the Grotto of the Sibyl, which you visit on the shoulders of a half-naked guide, with the delicious odor of torches smoking in the darkness. Or give me the solfatara (volcanic vent), spooky and suffocating, with its boiling mud simmering softly. Or the gardens, gardens upon gardens . . . I don't really like this country, but its gardens, draped in vines and roses and heavy with oranges, *are* delicious. And I have yet to see them in the summer! Naples and the bay . . . well, yes, of course, they're fine. But I've seen the bay, and that's enough. The sunrise is ravishing, but let's not make comparisons. There is something between this country and myself—an ancient grudge —which I cannot quite understand . . . I shall be in Paris about two Wednesday afternoon. I am not taking the boat. The sea is too choppy. My little companion* sends you his greetings. He is a sweet child when he is alone with me. But he will never be happy. His character is founded on a bottomless sadness.

André Rouveyre

Paris, January 9, 1911

I received the peas, fresh as rosebuds, and I ate a good part of them raw, because they were cold and sweet. We'll cook the rest. Thank you for having thought to send us something green and living. I had also received your letter, earlier, and it gave me a true, proud satisfaction.

Léon Hamel

Nice, February 14, 1911

It's raining, which should be enough to indicate my state of soul. I arrived by car from Beaulieu, where I spent several days. I don't like Beaulieu, or Nice either. Or Monte Carlo . . . where I have not yet entered the gaming rooms . . . Little Lily de Rême joined us a couple of days ago, and we make a trio which would interest you. These two children are odd by the very fact that they are both in love with me.

---

* Auguste Hériot, a wealthy young department-store heir who was close to Colette and Missy at this time. He is probably the model for Clouk, a character whom Colette eventually transformed into Chéri.

I gorge them and I put them to bed. My self-esteem takes maternal pride in their good appetites and fresh complexions. But I am not happy over the little Hériot . . . Our relationship seems to me serious above all for him. I myself am in no mortal danger. But I must talk to you about it. Upon which I have to unpack my bag again. Tonight I rehearse *Xantho*.

Yesterday I went to a matinee of *The Kreutzer Sonata*, with Suzanne Desprès and Lugné-Poë. What a pleasure it is not to have known such an interesting piece of work! And to prove how little a woman I am, let me tell you that from beginning to end I was *with* the man . . .

Claude Farrère*

Rozven, February 28, 1911

I am forced to move up my departure date for Tunis. I'll catch the *Carthage*, leaving Marseilles the 6th of March. Can you meet me there? I do hope so. It will console me at leaving this Brittany which is already adorable . . .

Thank you for having come to Toulon. I hug you and Missy shakes your hand.

Léon Hamel

Tunis, March 21, 1911

We've arrived in Zaghouan, exhausted, happy, and enchanted. But what a beautiful route: fifty kilometers of mountain road, through a sort of thorny brush, with camels passing by. And the springs, with such a pale, pure blue water, made to inspire thirst! Part of their flow goes to supply Tunis, and the rest waters the fields of mountain iris, flowering apricot trees, luminous green meadows, and olive groves. And yesterday we saw Sidi-bou-Saïd, a snowy-white village, entirely Arab, thank God, suspended above the sea. All goes well, though my face is brick-red.

* Claude Farrère (1876–1957), a naval officer who wrote novels with exotic backgrounds in the manner of Pierre Loti.

Missy tells me Auguste Hériot has arrived at Rozven, full of plaints and whimpers. Since my departure, I've left this little bird without a line, and it's very well that way . . .

Rozven, March 31, 1911

You must not be hurt if I passed through Paris without seeing you. I arrived Sunday morning in driving snow and rain and black cold . . . and I only saw the Sachas, who gave me a late supper. Missy was not pleased with my general state, but I'm better already, thanks to the truly surprising gentleness of the climate here. If you could see how rapidly spring is coming on! Thrift is already blossoming on the rocks, and the primroses abound. Missy has managed miracles and out of the chaos there is a room for me, and even one for her. There is still a lot to do, alas, and from time to time Missy gets discouraged. But she picks up again and work resumes. We eat anywhere, but the furnace works. I'll be back in Paris on the 13th, for two weeks . . . Then I'll tell you about the trip to Tunis, and how impossible Lily was, from Marseilles on. It was terrible! And when I think that she proposed our going to India together! I'd rather die . . .

Louis de Robert*

Rozven, early April 1911

. . . I'm finally emerging from my "vulgarity crisis." Sated, I have left the fake Midi and the companions who so strongly resembled this incurable ambient. From a distance, I now regard them with severity, as though I had never known them. They also escorted me to Tunis . . . where the souks are faked, and the merchants are scrupulously dressed up as Orientals and speak argot only to please the tourists. . . . Though I still have a cold, I am tasting all the joys for

---

* Louis de Robert (1871–1937), a novelist and journalist distinguished, in Colette annals, for having urged her to read Proust and given her a copy of *Swann's Way* inscribed: "To Madame Colette/ Admiring homage/ Marcel Proust."

which I was created, since I still deserve them. I wish you could see Rozven, with its cove of green sea, its complicated rocks, the little woods, the old and new trees, the warm terrace, the rosebushes, my yellow room, and the beach to which the tides bring treasures—mauve coral, polished shells, and sometimes casks of whale oil or benzine, from far-off shipwrecks. And I have a rocky perch, between the sky and the sea . . .

Georges Wague

Rozven, early May 1911

You can see that the Sacher paper is stunning. Naturally I've lost his address, so will you ask him to send me samples of his most lightweight papers, the sort used for foreign correspondence but not too transparent, which makes a pretty little metallic crackle when rubbed between the fingers. He'll surely know which I mean.

P.S. (personal) Ah! *mon petit*, what an arrival here! It's hard—it's arrangeable, but it's hard. I'll tell you all. But meantime write me asking if I'm available for rehearsals in Paris. Tell me that Pimples is free to rehearse from May 25 to June 2. Thanks.

Rozven, end of May 1911

Mon petit Brague, I've received your note. Everything is going much better here, thank God! I couldn't take any more, you know. I'll be in Paris in time, don't worry.

Anything new about the Gaîté-Rochechouart? Is the deal still on? And what will the definitive title be? Listen, since my first entrance onstage is after sunset, what if we called it *L'Oiseau de nuit*? It's not bad, and at least it's less vague than *Vagabonds*.

The trip was extraordinary. We looked as though we were playing a scene in an old Western. Our train caught fire three times, until finally there were real flames shooting through the ceiling and we were unloaded in the middle of a field, then reloaded in the baggage car. Naturally, we missed the connection at Rennes and were four hours late. But all's well now.

Rozven is so pretty! The Sachas are enchanted with the locality. Little Hériot is fine. He's telegraphed me twice; by now he must be in Oudjda, or somewhere else . . . Missy hugs you both: with the aid of a riding whip and ants' eggs, she is raising a five-day-old crow and a six-week-old finch. Pipo, the bulldog, is delicious.

Christiane Mendelys
Ouchy-Lausanne, July 2, 1911

Wague will give you all the latest news. Tell him for me that things are working out . . . only too well, and that Sidi* sings his praises and wants us all to be friends—the limit. Thanks for your own letter, as full of common sense as of affection. Wague can tell you that Missy's mental state had me rightly worried!

André Rouveyre
Paris, July 22, 1911

Your scrupulous and charming letter has touched me, extremely. Dear Rouveyre, you may write me and tell me everything you wish, without wounding or shocking me. Once and for all, I gave you the classification of *friend.* Use it.

Léon Hamel
Rozven, July 31, 1911

I am full of chagrin and remorse at having made you uneasy, and I have done as much to Mama and others who love me, in leaving them in ignorance as to my well-being.

* Family nickname for Henry de Jouvenel (1876–1935), journalist and editor of the prestigious newspaper *Le Matin,* who had entered Colette's life earlier in the year and who was presently to become her second husband.

But, dear Hamel, so much has been happening! I have suffered—it being necessary to pay for happiness (touch wood)—yes, or at least something resembling happiness, which I can now see shining within my reach (I touch wood again, frantically).

I arrived at Rozven this morning, after a very agitated month, which I spent almost entirely in Paris, and in a mortal heat wave. You know that I played *La Chair* in Geneva and Lausanne? But do you know that, the day after his duel, Jouvenel arrived in Lausanne, wounded and with his arm in a sling, declaring that he neither could nor would live without me? Do you know that at the same time Hériot wanted to join me in Switzerland, and that I prevented him from doing so with a series of crazy, lying, and contradictory telegrams? Do you know that, on returning to Paris, Jouvenel admitted to La Panthère that he loved another woman? Upon which she declared that she would kill this woman, no matter who she might be. Desperate, Jouvenel transmitted this threat, upon which I replied: "I'm going to see her." And I went. And I told La Panthère, "I'm the woman." Upon which she melted and entreated me. But her contrition was short-lived, for two days later she announced to Jouvenel her intention to knife me. Desperate again, Jouvenel had me picked up by Sauerwein in a car, and, still with Sauerwein, accompanied me to Rozven. Here we found Missy glacial and disgusted, having just received news of what was happening from La Panthère. Then my two guardians left me and Paul Barlet mounted guard, with a revolver, no less. Missy, still glacial and disgusted, flew the coop and went to Honfleur. Three days later, Jouvenel summoned me back to his side by telephone, and Sauerwein came to pick me up by car, because La Panthère was out on the prowl, looking for me and armed with a revolver. Here began my period of semi-sequestration in Paris, where I was guarded like a precious reliquary by the Sûreté as well as by Jouvenel, Sauerwein, and Sapène, three pillars of *Le Matin*. And believe me or not, this period has just come to an end, thanks to an unex-

pected, providential, and magnificent event! Tired of waiting around, Mr. Hériot—if you please!—and Madame la
Panthère—no less!—have just embarked on his yacht, the
Esmerald, for a six-week cruise, after having astonished Le
Havre, their home port, with their drunken orgies. Is that
good? Is it good theater? Just a little too much, wouldn't
you say?

Meantime, Jouvenel distinguished himself by very proper
behavior, which earned him the disesteem of Missy: for
Missy, basically, adores Hériot. She had even prepared him
a room here at Rozven, and she intended to impose him
on me quasi-conjugally. That's all I needed to disgust me
with this young man forever.

What else is there to tell you, dear Hamel? Jouvenel is
arranging his Paris house for us. He has no money except his
salary at *Le Matin* (forty thousand francs), but since I earn
my own comfortable living, we can manage. Do I have to tell
you that I love this man, who is tender, jealous, unsociable,
and incurably honest? Hardly necessary. But I do very much
want to see you. And I *shall* see you often, if you consent,
since Jouvenel has already declared that he will permit me
only "Hamel and Barlet." There!

I am also happy to report that Sapène showed himself,
toward both Jouvenel and myself, an incomparable friend.
It was a very agreeable surprise.

Missy has meantime bought Princesse, the villa three
kilometers away. This makes a sort of epilogue, doesn't it?
Though Missy is still glacial and disgusted, and no matter
what I do, I can't get a sensible word out of her . . . The
day after tomorrow I leave for Castel-Novel, the Jouvenel
family château in the Corrèze. I'll send you a photograph . . .

André Rouveyre

Hôtel Meurice, Paris, August 25, 1911

You will not see Missy with me again, *cher ami*. We are no
longer living together. I'll explain everything when you wish
—it's so simple . . .

Christiane Mendelys

Hôtel Meurice, Paris, August 29, 1911

But who told you that I have been neglecting physical culture? I just have a new method, that's all. The Sidi Method. It's excellent. But no public courses. Only private lessons . . . extremely private. . . . News of Missy? I have none, and she continues to detain all my belongings. But I am very pleased to have an exception made for me: I shall be the first to have seen La Marquise ask for money from a woman she has left . . .

Léon Hamel

Paris, September 20, 1911

. . . Nothing new here. We still do not have a bedroom, but a tenacious hope sustains us. Sidi is fine . . . I cannot hide from you the fact that I am mightily attached to him . . .

André Rouveyre

57, rue Cortambert, Paris, November 8, 1911

Here is the address of my new home. At this moment I am in bed with bronchitis, but I'll be better, surely.

Léon Hamel

Villerville, May 13, 1912

We're on our way home from Trouville, which I didn't know. Sidi has been showing me around this elegant necropolis, where at this time of year you see only dogs and an occasional mason. Properly to appreciate the funereal charm of the *rue de Paris*, one would have to know the Trouville of August and Suzanne Derval. Normandy itself is a delicious country—when you first see it. But I doubt if its soft green charms and its tiresome humidity would hold my interest as long as they have that of our fickle Sacha, who has been a fixture of Honfleur for so long. My best moments have been walking in the woods, where one is barely conscious of the sea . . . We are eating a great deal and very well. I'm gaining weight and Sidi is already vigorously tanned and revoltingly young.

We leave tomorrow, planning to have lunch in Rouen and dinner in Paris. We'll see. Does my letter smell of garlic? I've just had a bread crust rubbed with olive oil, garlic, and salt . . .

Angers, June 16, 1912

I arrived here yesterday evening, having barely passed through town on my way. Nevertheless, there was time for an odd crisis with Sidi. It's too difficult to describe just now. I'll tell you about it in person. It does not take very long to make oneself ill with chagrin, as you know. We separated feeling very reconciled, but still . . . I'll be back Tuesday morning. It's windy here and I'm afraid there may be accidents . . .*

Tours, June 26, 1912

. . . If you see Paul Barlet, he will tell you what strange days I've been living through, and what the effect can be on a man without willpower when he gets what he wants and what he wants is a definitive separation. Four days of conversation boil down to something like this:

Jouvenel: We have to separate.
Colette: Yes!
J.: Life together . . .
C.: . . . is impossible.
J.: That wouldn't prevent our remaining good friends!
C.: On the contrary!
J.: So we are going to separate . . .
C.: At once!

---

* Colette was in Angers to attend the Grand Prix d'Aviation. Under the dateline of June 13, she had described her ascent in a dirigible in Paris. See *Contes des mille et un matins.*

J.: Oh! there's no need to hurry.

C.: Yes, yes, it's absolutely urgent.

J.: Absolute is hardly the word . . .

C.: Absolute! The first of July we'll make a clean break. Each will go his own way. If, for my part, there is an emotional change, that is to say, if I meet someone beddable and friendly, then simple loyalty would make it my duty . . .

J.: Certainly. But meanwhile . . .

C.: Meanwhile, I move to Paul Barlet's in the rue La Fontaine.

J.: That's unnecessary, and even stupid. You're better off here.

C.: No. Good night, Sidi.

J.: But . . . Where are you going?

C.: Where I belong. You yourself have told me . . .

J.: Oh, well! What I've said is not of great importance . . . Wouldn't you like to play a game of cards?

C.: Cards? With pleasure.

J.: . . . Four thousand five hundred!

C.: Bravo! Upon which . . . adieu, Sidi.

J.: But . . . what are you doing this evening? If it wouldn't revolt you to have dinner chez Laurent in the open air, the weather is good, and I'd so much like to stay with you . . . Etc., etc.

I am showing you, dear Hamel, the comic side. Unhappily, there are others. But I've passed the dead point. Meantime, Sauerwein, very appropriately, has sent me here to cover the Guillotin trial.* I arrived yesterday evening. The legal press flutters around me, Henri de Robert has adopted me, and all goes well. Sidi took me to the railway station looking like a lost dog. I don't despair of treating him as frivolously as I did Hériot.

I'll be coming back Saturday, probably . . . I count on you unendingly. And I comfort myself with the thought that

* Colette's account of this murder trial is in *Contes des mille et un matins.*

I shall need you. No one, at this moment, is closer to me than you.

Villerville-sur-mer, July 10, 1912
I'm not in such capital shape right now, but a dreadful bitterness is beginning to grow in me, and I count on it for comfort—yes, a dreadful bitterness against the sort of wretch who can neither take care of nor defend a woman . . . The weather is fine, but I'm dying of physical fatigue without being able to sleep, and I do not want to go on feeling so inferior. Alas, I miss the *presence* of an unworthy being terribly—miss his warmth, the sound of his voice, his lies, his childish and ridiculous behavior. But you're not someone I have to explain that to . . .

Paris, July 20, 1912
All I can find in the way of stationery is this half-mourning paper, which is, after all, quite "adequate" to the situation. Yes, yes, I know perfectly well that I must have a place of my own. But at this moment I can't possibly manage it. I have fifteen hundred francs, including payment today from *Le Matin*. That's not enough to move, or set up an apartment, or even travel.

The 31st of August, Jouvenel is to pay me a thousand francs, but that's the 31st of August. From now until then I'll earn another twenty-five louis . . . In September I'll make 1,400 francs for an engagement at the Bataclan, and I'll also be paid for a little deluxe volume which Paul Barlet and his friend are bringing out. So, until there's a change, I'll go on living chez Jouvenel. We are on "good terms." On his part (I'm telling you everything) there is even a carnal tenacity that is very odd. Since I am prone for my part to the same tyranny, I conclude that there are good moments and bad quarters of an hour. But this must not go on for very long, and I'll keep you informed as to my progress as well as my lapses, very dear Hamel.

I have gone back to *Le Raisin volé*, and this time I hope it will work. As soon as everything is settled regarding the volume *Prrou, Poucette et quelques autres*, I'll leave town, and stay with either Georges Wague or Jean Sapène. But it's raining terribly, and bless me, I don't want to get interned chez Sapène at this point! . . . I'm playing the piano— working on some little bits of Schumann which ought to please you and which you won't recognize. I'm also "plotting" . . . You'll know what. It's only a matter of an attempt at evasion . . . sensual evasion, that is. It would be useful.

Paris, August 6, 1912

. . . Jouvenel left the first of the month for his aviation week at Brive, and we parted very agreeably. He asked me to over- see the interior decoration still in progress at the house, as though I were going to finish my days here. And I have done so, as well as taken care of other matters, not concern- ing him. I have pawned my pearls, for instance, putting them in the hands of the one person—Auguste Hériot—who can discreetly assure me a decent price. I am thus guarantee- ing myself immediate liberty—I can pull out in two hours if I wish to. But I don't wish to. I am still waiting. Today I am writing to the "baron," who is putting on a show and going into debt in Brive. But don't worry, I'm not offering him money . . .

Unlike you, Sauerwein thinks I should end the situation at once. He and Sapène were shocked when they found that Jouvenel and I were still living together and moreover were perfectly good-humored about it. At Sapène's indignation, Jouvenel replied: "What of it, after all? Colette is not so badly off where she is. And neither am I."

Paris, August 17, 1912

. . . The news I have for you today will not make you un- happy. Jouvenel returned at midnight Monday. At first, he was amiable and defiant, then very brusquely he became a man who has just awakened and is astonished to find he was asleep. His manner and language revealed an egoism so naïve and so childish that I wanted to laugh and cry at once. He assured me that I had "changed" . . . Though which of us has really changed, it would be hard to say. Will the change last? I am not so crazy as to hope that it will, dear Hamel. But I am letting myself enjoy a rough, ephemeral happiness, which will have a price. You understand how important the *presence* of the necessary being can be after hours and weeks. Now he is arranging "our" future with the same eagerness as he arranges the bibelots on the dresser.

Georges Wague

Paris, August 26, 1912

. . . I should be very happy to go to Roumania for ten days, providing my well-known cupidity is satisfied. Can you make out the foolish smile on my face? It's because I am happy. There are some squalls which are beneficial, and I think I have just survived one that is not ordinary. But I should be lying if I said I am going to visit you. I am going to visit Châtillon, where my sainted mother is insupportable. Not that she is seriously ill, but she's having a crisis of "I wish to see my daughter." Sidi is allowing me three days—at the maximum . . .

Léon Hamel

Paris, August 27, 1912

. . . I'm leaving for Châtillon, but only for forty-eight hours. I shall be returning at noon Friday . . . I have only excellent news to give you: the "return" is so complete, and at the same time so bizarre and so justified . . .

Christiane Mendelys

Châtillon-Coligny, August 29, 1912

Yes, Brague told me, you have lost your brother all of a sudden. I should have written you sooner, though you are one of those who do not take silence for indifference. I assume you are enduring your grief in your own manner, that is, without saying anything and with an everyday face, the way courageous people do, for whom loss is not a novelty. Your letter caught up with me here, where I am only staying forty-eight hours—Sidi thinks that a quite sufficient time to be away, which fact alone will shed light on our present relations . . .

Georges Wague

Paris, early September 1912

. . . A small concession for Budapest? But how much? If I agree to lower my fee by two louis, that would be the absolute maximum. People who have been there tell me the cost of living is very high. It seems that Russia is impossible . . . Nothing very new here: happy people have no story. Mornings we go horseback riding together and I have a wonderful time. Sidi is a love as never before!

Léon Hamel

Paris, September 17, 1912

. . . Just to tell you that "everything is going fine" in and around me. Poor Hamel, how I have tormented you with my miseries! But be assured: I am a pear that has survived a hailstorm: when it does not rot, it becomes better and sweeter than the others, in spite of its little scars. It's midnight. Sidi is still at *Le Matin*. When you are back you'll see how handsome the little kittens are becoming . . .

Paris, September 27, 1912

. . . Mama died the day before yesterday. I don't want to go to the burial. I shall wear no visible mourning, and I am telling almost no one. But I am tormented by the stupid notion that I shall no longer be able to write to her as I always have. I am continuing to perform *L'Oiseau* and to

live as usual. But as always when I am suffering emotionally,
I am having an attack of internal inflammation which is very
painful . . .

Castel-Novel, Corrèze, October 14, 1912

I have been installed at Castel-Novel since my arrival, and
everyone is charming to me. My mother-in-law, as Sidi says,
is youth itself. Then there is his brother, Robert, and a
younger sister, who is a gentle, giant child bearing a striking
resemblance to Sidi. There is also a classic and kind English
governess who gets up in the middle of the night—I don't
exaggerate—to bring me aspirin. Finally there is a bright,
roasting sun, which is drying out my filthy cold, and then the
château itself, entirely worthy of the surrounding landscape. But this life of "country rest" would exhaust even the
heartiest souls, and everyone goes to bed early. And by eight
in the morning everyone is up again and on the move: Sidi
to the farm, his mother to the tennis court, myself here
and there. The day before yesterday we went on an excursion
to Curemonte, a nearby château which Robert has bought
and which will need one hundred thousand francs' worth of
repairs before one can even dream of furnishing it. Yesterday we spent the day at Castelnau, a splendid estate which
has been lovingly restored and filled with marvels by the
tenor Jean Mouliérat. Oh, Hamel, what a château! with
African terraces where vanilla beans, monstrous grapes, and
pomegranates are ripening side by side . . .

Lac Leman, October 30, 1912

. . . We're on a boat touring the lake. We set out with the
laudable if funereal intention of paying a visit to Madame
Picard in Lausanne, but by the time we reached Ouchy, I
felt myself overwhelmed by a vast despondency and a deep
desire to stay on the boat with Wague and Kerf, to relax and
watch the water and think as little as possible. Which is just
what I am doing, without the least remorse. I shall send a

telegram to the incandescent Swiss lady and blame it all
on . . . the child.

> *Paris, December 7, 1912*
Dear Hamel, it is absolutely inexcusable for me to have
forgotten the Reboux dinner . . . the invitation to which we
had accepted on the 28th. Sidi has cursed me out roundly!
But leave the number of your loge at the box office, and I'll
join you after dinner. We are to be married on the 19th at
4:30. But at the registry one has to give one's age!!! It's
fantastic but obligatory.

Christiane Mendelys

> *Paris, December 27, 1912*
My little Croppy, how sweet of you to write me. You ask
what I'm doing? The answer is, I'm getting bigger, very
slowly but surely. I feel pregnant above all in the evening—
about eight o'clock not a dress or a belt seems to fit—*he*
has to have room, and he has his way. You see how he already resembles his father. Apart from this . . . we've been
on a spree since the 18th. We were married the 19th, and
since then the staff and friends of *Le Matin* have passed us
from table to table, from lunch to dinner to supper, even on
Christmas eve, after which we wound up our week of dis-
soluteness by getting to bed at 7 a.m. If this child isn't the
wildest rake, I give up!

Georges Wague

> *Paris, late January 1913*
. . . I've just finished a week of enteritis . . . and we're leav-
ing tomorrow for the Midi. Sidi needs the change as much as
I. His kidneys are bruised and his head overworked. I ex-
pect to relax for eight days and make progress on my
novel. We return on the 11th, as Sidi has a lecture at
Limoges on the 13th. I myself am giving one on Backstage
Music-Hall Life in Nice on the 9th. My "litter" keeps mov-

ing. It behaves in a waggish manner, lively and knowing what it's up to, like an adult playing a hoax. The effect is very bizarre . . .

Léon Hamel

Nice, February 6, 1913

. . . If we continue to relax in this manner, we'll come home on stretchers. I'm exaggerating very little. Everything distracts us: the brisk, cloudless weather, the desire to be on the move, the Polignacs' automobile, the need to be in two places at once, Sidi's youthful appetite for life, which has taken less than forty-eight hours to give him a farmer's tan, broiled cheeks, and a vermilion nose. Last night he went all alone to the carnival, amused himself like a god, and came home at 5 a.m., ravished and satiated at having clasped so many anonymous behinds. Meantime He—or She-whom-I'm-carrying-in-my-flanks . . . bounds up and down, until I wonder if I'm going to give birth to a Monegasque goat. . . . The friendly Polignacs take us everywhere in their car. Tomorrow we are to see the aquarium, and in the evening, after dining with the director of the Nice Opéra, we are to see *Siegfried* . . . The Mortola Gardens were closed today: and I wanted to steal a digitated lemon leaf!

Georges Wague

Paris, March 1913

No, *mon vieux*, relax, there is no hitch, everything is going fine, it's only that at the end of a day my mug droops, and this gives me an even more interesting air . . . Only my novel torments me. I feel so hand-to-mouth . . .

Christiane Mendelys

Paris, May 1, 1913

I'm leaving, we're leaving tomorrow morning at eight. I've been on the run all day and I must work on *L'Entrave* in order to give Saglio his copy . . .

Léon Hamel

Castel-Novel, May 3, 1913

I had the *Cahiers d'aujourd'hui* before leaving. The article was indeed charming. Since we arrived, it has been raining in an unbelievable and offensive manner. And Robert is bedridden with a fever brought back from the Congo. He is to be injected with quinine. The rest of us—all three of us—are very well, and this diluvial sky is forcing me to work . . .

Castel-Novel, May 9, 1913

. . . For two days it's been June, with all the roses in bloom, and Sidi "plotting" all over the place—the least of the changes he dreams of for his lands and his castle would stagger the imagination!

Paul Barlet*

Paris, mid-June 1913

. . . Here is the copy for Saglio. He needs twenty-two to twenty-five pages of my holograph manuscript for one issue. So he has enough now for two numbers. And now stir your stumps! (I have a certain cheek, no doubt!) I'm giving this note to Sidi. Tomorrow I'll write again . . . but this evening I can only cry "Hang it all!" I have now begun the ending for the third time! And why don't you want me to use the word *imperméabilité*? *Obscurité* might be possible, but all the others are too weak. After all, it is Jean who is speaking . . . I won't look at it again this evening, though. Meantime, long live repeated words! Shall I have proofs?

Georges Wague

Paris, mid-July 1913

I have a little Rat,† and I have paid the price: thirty hours *without* respite, chloroform and forceps. She is pretty and

* Paul Barlet, for years Willy's secretary, remained a loyal friend to Colette after the divorce. Later he was the publisher of *L'Entrave*.
† Colette de Jouvenel, otherwise known as Bel-Gazou, was born in Paris on July 3, 1913.

well built, she has long eyes and a head covered with hair.
Since the delivery, I have been mending as if by magic, to
the doctor's amazement. I eat sitting up, and I should be
back on my feet in eight days. Sidi is wild about his
daughter . . .

Louis Barthou*

Paris, July 18, 1913

Here is an "early version" of *La Vagabonde*, which, as you
can see, was originally to have been an epistolary novel.
But this experiment limited itself to fifty pages . . .

I have a pretty little daughter fourteen days old.

Léon Hamel

Castel-Novel, August 10, 1913

My daughter is charming and very resourceful for her age.
My mother-in-law is charming too, and barely any older
than my daughter . . . Sidi has been sporting a little fever
for the past forty-eight hours, but it's nothing. He caught
cold in the car. His tribe of females is nursing him with
doting love.

Castel-Novel, September 16, 1913

Hamel! dear Hamel! Fruit-bearing Hamel! Pleasing and
discreet Hamel! I have finished *L'Entrave*. I exult with relief, but I despise and vomit the result.

Since you left, my life has been made up of hard work and
facile vanities. The latter have been presidential and re-
publican. I have had the joy of hearing Sidi and Poincaré
acclaimed. Luncheon with the President and his wife at
Brive (Madame Poincaré is charming, and wants a blue cat).
Culinary expositions, a dinner, with myself as hostess, for
eighty-seven guests, reception at the Geographic Society,
everything, everything. And during all this time I have been

---

* Louis Barthou (1862–1934), a politician and bibliophile who, as
Minister of Foreign Affairs, was assassinated in Marseilles in October
1934.

trying to find a synonym for *avid*. Don't look, Hamel. There isn't one—or at least not the one I want.

At present, I am sociable, attentive to conversation, very nice, and futile. Soon I am going to be able to crochet and go horseback riding . . . The day before I finished *L'Entrave*, I worked six hours. The last day, eleven hours. As the end was no good, I had to begin all over. I confess this with shame, since the result does not correspond with my tardy efforts. I thank you infinitely for the fruits, especially the figs, which were a great success . . .

Paris, October 4, 1913

. . . the wet-nurse lost her milk, and since the 24th I've been in Paris, scouring placement bureaus for another nurse, English or otherwise. It's all been odious, I assure you. Anguish, anxiety, and boredom . . .

Castel-Novel, November 19, 1913

Dear Hamel, first the most urgent news: my daughter is magnificent. She's a ruddy little replica of Sidi, tyrannical, with a handsome, vigorous body. But my Lord, how little one knows oneself. I arrived here in perfect tranquillity. I found the little one in the salon—and all at once I had burst into tears! Doubtless it's very natural, but I was surprised. I had found her so beautiful. She has a charming character, with brusque turns of temper which promptly give way to smiles. And she has a reassuring gaiety. I hope a photograph in which she is lovingly holding her bottle *herself* comes out. She is calm, and sits up straight (because her nurse insists). She knows that she has two ears, because after one has been cleaned, she offers the other. She also holds up her hand to put on a sleeve. All this is slight, yet at the same time an index of a quick intelligence, since she is only five months old. She has black lashes, eyes the color of a stormy sea, a very beautiful color, which will doubtless change, unhappily. Can you imagine my ever being bored with such a child? Sidi dotes on her.

And now, dear Hamel, I shall give you the true and staggering truth about the weather we're having. This morning—November 19th—I had my bath in front of an open window!

Marguerite Moreno

Paris, February 11, 1914

Listen, to hell with Molière! That's all I really wanted to say this afternoon. I have a horror of speaking about something I know nothing about. I had an excellent reception . . . but Sidi was in the audience, which was enough to demoralize me. At the end I gave way to an excess of sincerity, and dared to admit that I could live without Molière and that his lines were not sufficiently beautiful and sonorous for my taste. Ouf! That's over . . .

My dear child, I know the Oceanographic Museum at Monaco better than you. There used to be a tank of snake-fish that gave me gooseflesh, and as for the octopus, I was afraid to bathe after seeing it, lest it turn up in the hotel bathtub.

Yesterday evening, chez Natalie Clifford Barney, there were two Englishwomen—a couple, it seemed to me—who were worth seeing. But how we all miss you—Sidi, Barthou, Robert d'Humières, and Colette! (I hear a cyclone approaching—a *cyclone*, that is. I barely have the time to fold up my table and cede him the vast workroom-bathroom where I operate.) . . . Sidi is handsome, glorious, and imperious as ever.

Paris, March 1914

You're writing? While waiting to admire you, I feel a somber joy, and say to myself: "She too. Now she too knows what it is to be desperate over a word instead of toasting in the sun. Now she too gnaws the tip of her pen and tears up pages . . ." (When you need more paper, let me know.)

I'm disgusted with dress rehearsals if you're not there. The end of the afternoon often seems cruel. I tell myself,

"What have I failed to do? Oh, yes! I haven't gone to see Moreno."

Paris, March 8, 1914

. . . Did you get my postcards from Belgium? I thought I'd caught my death of cold while I was there. This in spite of the fact that I inaugurated a very new treatment: at Anvers I took a two-hour walk on the waterfront in a pelting rain. The results, at first sight—or for that matter, at second or third sight—were hardly what I expected.

We came back day before yesterday and I still have my lousy paper to do for *Le Matin*. Last night I saw *Georgette Lemeunier*, with a good little debutante—a bit dry still, not rounded off at the edges, but a good sort, it seemed to me. But what about your book?

Léon Hamel

Castel-Novel, March 14, 1914

My daughter enchants me. She's a big farm girl, ruddy, plump, gay, with an eye full of vivacity and variety. She flirts with any male who comes along—the gardener, the telegraph boy, the mason. She looks like both Sidi and me. She has a superbly robust little body, very well made, hard thighs and calves, aggressive buttocks, and a pair of shoulders which will surely be beautiful. She is blond— imagine!—but the nurse assures us this is only a passing thing. An unqualifiable cheek: like a bulldog, she is afraid of nothing. When you take her thumb out of her mouth, she gives you a punch, but then promptly acquiesces. Hair as flat as her mother's, alas, not the least curl. But she is very much the king of the cats, with her lock on one side.

What else? A radiant morning and a lamentable afternoon, with a driving rain. Why aren't you here with me, in front of this wood fire, playing a sharp game of bezique?

There are millions of violets, but everything else is still sleeping.

Castel-Novel, May 6, 1914

. . . The month of May is intoxicating, and what wild orchids, almost a meter high, deep purple, growing in the meadows; and roses and medlar trees in blossom. The white rose vine covering the front of the château is so white with flowers that at night it seems to trace a milky way. And the nightingales don't seem to have time to either eat or drink, since they sing from four in the afternoon to seven in the morning and from four in the morning to four in the afternoon. When, I wonder, do they make love?

Georges Wague

Paris, summer 1914

. . . Don't curse us. The cook leaves for Rozven tomorrow, ahead of us by several hours (if you think one can write legibly with a Brazilian squirrel on one's arm!). I'll pick up Sidi at *Le Matin* at midnight and off we'll go, by car, as long as Saint-Pneu permits!

Now listen! I've seen d'Estournelles de Constant and things look good for you . . . I've also written Fauré . . .

Léon Hamel

Rozven, July 15, 1914

How beautiful it is here . . . and what a good life, without shoes, in the water or on the sand most of the time . . . Sidi is discovering life at the seaside and he can't be dragged out of the water. He goes in without a bathing suit—so much for modesty!—and rolls in the sand and cannot be consoled for having to return to Paris this evening . . .

Rozven, August 1, 1914

. . . with the heat there has been a hatching of Vulcain butterflies and of little tortoises, cool, lively, of an unblemished velvet, which would delight you. The weather has been Rozven weather, that is, never cold, often stormy, dead calm without rain, or scorching hot with a light wind—deliciously variable. After the high tides, the sea has been thick with large and small jellyfish, of translucent crystal, starred with russet brown and fringed with brownish-black—marvels which would especially gratify you by the mild, blistering discharge they emit. I have spent the past fortnight alone with Musi, who makes very sweet and easy company. But Sidi arrives tomorrow, and would you believe it, I'm not put out! If it can be of any interest to you, Hamel, I have also been working out patiently and regained my old muscles: thanks not only to physical culture but to raking, waxing floors, and carrying heavy loads. I've done it all and am now in shape, formidably, to take on any match you wish.

Sidi writes me this morning that he still believes peace is possible, and that the attitude of Paris, uneasy but excited and swaggering, is not unpleasing . . .

Christiane Mendelys

Paris, August 30, 1914

Sidi is at Verdun, alas. I am as patient, as gay and as reasonable as I can be, and as I owe it to him to be. Like everyone, I am almost without money, and little Musi and I are living here together. She's broke too, and does the marketing and a lot of other chores. My daughter is in Rozven, thank God, and in splendid shape . . . When I am *obliged to*, I'll leave Paris—where I can still write little things for *Le Matin*—and join her there. You realize that Sidi is not on any "journalistic mission." He's a sub-lieutenant in the 44th. Our income is thus extremely reduced. And it is probable that as the Germans get closer and closer to Paris the newspapers will stop appearing altogether and be replaced by an officially printed bulletin from the War Ministry. But I am not complaining. I've just had three letters from Sidi, delivered by military personnel on a mission. I embrace both of you, my dears, and I envy little Croppy for having her man near her. It's been almost a month since I've seen mine.

Léon Hamel

Paris, September 18, 1914

Fighting for three days near Verdun, Sidi saw an ordnance officer, his companion, killed at his side. He jumped at the impact, fell into a ditch, and hurt his foot. Already cured, alas, he is back under fire. He had had no news of the world or me since September 4. Neither newspapers nor communiqués. The underground telegram had only alerted them of the German withdrawal from Paris. From the 5th to the 10th the battle around Verdun did not let up for an hour's truce. His accident was on the 8th; I had his letter the 16th . . . Tell this to Missy, will you? She sets a high value on courage, and I don't want to lose any occasion to be proud of Sidi . . .

Paris, September 27, 1914

If you come back to Paris in October, would you have the kindness to bring Baghera and Ricotte with you? Naturally I'll pay for Baghera's ticket (you'll keep her on her leash with a very tight collar). Ricotte will be in her cage, with a few nuts and crusts, and you'll only have to give her a drink now and then on the trip, from a glass or the hollow of your hand.

Two or three unimportant bombs this morning. One of them fell near here and I had a look at it. It looks like a machine made expressly to frighten people. This particular one nearly hit the town house of Madame de Comminges, but even if it had, it would barely have staved in the roof.

Sidi? He's fighting. As I permitted myself to write him that it would be agreeable for me if he were here, and that *Le Matin*, my God, constituted an important facet of his Duty (in his absence *Le Matin* has nearly been suppressed), he replied with a patriotic lecture. Can you see him, on his horse, above the smoke of battle? God is mighty who can make such soldiers . . .

Paris, October 16, 1914

. . . I have begun my duties as a night watchman at Janson. It's a terrible job and I am not surprised that it's not in great demand. Thirteen hours on the alert, and *all* the patients' needs to be looked after. When morning arrives, one is a bit haggard. But beginning next week the night service will be taken over by male nurses, and I'll have a daytime job.

. . . Nothing unusual here. It's raining. From time to time we have a few dirigibles, but I cannot accustom myself to paying any more attention to them than to a storm cloud overhead. Alas, dear Hamel, it's been 64 days since I've seen Sidi!

Verdun, December 20, 1914

Since this morning, we've had the most beautiful cannonade, an uninterrupted tempest, with doors rattling and windows tinkling. Now it's nightfall, and I have just been to the citadel, high up, to see what can be seen of a fogbound battle five kilometers away. That is to say, our cannons are five kilometers away!

That puts the enemy troops about eighteen or nineteen kilometers away. The mist, the nighttime, the pink flashes from the cannons, and other brief bursts of aurora borealis in the distance. Ah! If I could only climb high in the daylight with a good pair of binoculars! But it's forbidden. I'd be sent away within twenty-four hours. So I resign myself with joy to my prisoner's life here.

Sidi is fine, his joy seems as great as my own, and I ask for nothing more. There is little or no talk of war here. Hardly anyone looks at a newspaper. The following dialogue is accurate.

—Have you heard the news?

—They've just received a shipment of first-rate sauerkraut.

—Is that possible?

—Just as I say!

And then when the zeppelins are passing over, you hear someone crying out:

—In the name of God, these pigs have a mania for dropping their waste matter at just the time when I'm out looking for butter . . .

This is exact: there is no more urgent or serious question than nutrition. I shall write some sketches about this later on.

At night I go out along the Meuse River. From the bridge, I can make out the water, the hospital, the fortress, the barrage in the distance. That's all, but that's enough. In the evening, Sidi comes home to his harem. Behind closed venetian blinds or darkened doors, I can make out other cloistered women like myself—one of them fearfully taking a little fresh air on her threshold. One doesn't otherwise know that they are here, and by day, their men, like mine, go to their posts with an indifferent air. The hardiest emerge at twilight, for a little while, like bats. I have many reasons to remember forever the days I am spending here.

Verdun, February 4, 1915

I am not just using a figure of speech when I say that I have passed through enemy bombs to come back here and write you this. What an experience!

The weather was springlike, so we went out—Louise Lamarque, her dog, and I—following the towpath, where one only encounters boatmen. At five hundred meters from the town, an antiaircraft barrage began, and we could admire the zeppelin overhead, with the blossoming in the air around him of ten, twenty round tufts, tiny, bright, motionless; exploding shells being fired at him. The arrival of pursuing planes, the appearance of another zeppelin, were all clearly visible in the air, so clean, so legible, so beautiful that we'd have only felt enthusiasm for the show if . . . if the

height of the battle had not suddenly passed over us . . .
We took refuge under an iron bridge, with shells falling
three meters away but fizzling out in the water like torches.
I was worried because I knew that for the least scratch I
would be confined to the house or sent back to Paris. A
bomb fell on the neighboring meadow, but without exploding, since the ground was so waterlogged. The barrage
shook the stomach, and overhead white bouquets continued
to blossom . . . but I thought of the fortress where Sidi
was working. Finally, the soldiers gave us a sign to leave the
bridge, since the battle was moving away. Going home, we
saw a bomb crater on the quai, and at the station we were
told that a man had been cut in half. Then at home, there
was a bomb in the garden . . . Finally, the last and irri-
tating effect of the bombardment has been a cutoff of our
electricity. We have four candles for the entire house . . .

Rome, June 28, 1915

Thanks to Boni de Castellane, who is leaving for Paris
this evening, you'll have this note before my postcards. I'll
never have the time to write you a real letter. People have
been very charming to me here, though Madame Boas
[Jouvenel's first wife] came close to making Rome uninhabitable. On her recent visit here, she assumed the name
she still loves so well. I arrive under this same name—
naturally—and I am taken for an impersonator-adventuress.
That mix-up was soon resolved, except at the Hotel Ex-
celsior, *her* hotel, where I was not received. What do you
say to that? My own forbearance is rapidly running out.

As for Rome, I'm trying to gobble up as much as possible,
though without collapsing in this African heat. The staff of
the French embassy is charming, and praise the Lord,
M. de Billy is nothing like what I was told he would be.

Hamel, I'm sick of Basilicas. I detest St. Peter's and Santa
Maria Maggiore and if St. John Lateran didn't have its

cloister . . . Apart from that, there are a hundred things which enchant me . . . Do you know Santa Maria in Cosmedin? And then what gardens! what palace courtyards, each one with its own fountain, and almost every one of them beautiful, or seductive. But I've only seen a sampling of it all, even of the Roman campagna . . . There's also D'Annunzio, who is much more agreeable in Rome than in Paris—we have neighboring apartments.

What saddens me is the paucity of news from Sidi. All his letters are opened, censored, and delayed. The day after tomorrow, I'll be in Venice. We're forbidden to go there, but I've been able to see the chief of police, and obtained a five-day pass, the maximum . . .

Lago di Como, September 22, 1916
. . . We're having a tempest, Hamel, the kind we used to have at Crotoy! The lake is covered with whitecaps, and all the boats are anchored or pulled up out of the water. I would never have thought an Italian lake capable of such wrath. And a wind—as though we were facing the open sea. Otherwise, all is well, and I'm writing articles for *La Vie Parisienne* . . .

Rome, January 7, 1917
. . . If you see Annie, she can tell you that, apart from museums and churches, my life here isn't so different from the one I lead in Paris: Borghese Gardens in the morning with the dogs, and if he has the time, Sidi rejoins us at noon. He doesn't have the time just now: the French government is here en masse, and Sidi is overwhelmed.

Hamel, the Villa Borghese in the Roman winter is like the Bois de Boulogne in May. What a winter it is which invites us to have lunch out of doors under the trees! It would take me a long time to feel blasé about that. And the oak trees in perennial leaf, and the umbrella pines . . . But there is no bucolic life without cream cheese; I eat it all day. One has to reinforce the wartime hotel menu a bit. The decrees forbid cheese at table, and butter as well, and permit only two dishes per meal—soup and salad each counting as a dish, and sugar in tiny sacks of fifteen and twenty grams, etc. Everything is not roses in the tourist life of chic hotels these days!

Rome, March 22, 1917

. . . yes, I have been treating you in a very nearly disgusting manner. To my natural laziness, destiny has added that of Rome. Oh, Hamel, when one sees the Roman buildings, even damaged as they are by time, when one sees the present-day Romans, and feels oneself softened, sweetened, made sanguine by this deadly, incomparable climate, one wonders: "How on earth did the ancient Romans do all that they did?" I swear to you that it's a stupefying question.

. . . What else can I tell you? Sidi is much more courageous than I, who am lazily scissoring away at texts for *Les Heures longues*. I'm also waiting for Musi, and I'll have to remain on here another month because of the film version of *La Vagabonde* she is going to make. Meantime, I have appeared at the British embassy—who gave a charity matinee—reading three of my *Dialogues de bêtes*, which had a distinct success . . .

I have a new refuge—the Palatine Hill. Springtime is wild there, and I can pick white narcissus in the fields without being disturbed. There are anemones we don't have in France—purple, pale pink, immense, charming—and large clusters of wild mignonette, and the kind of orchids we have in Brittany. For an entire week I haven't encountered another soul there. But, apart from flowers, everything is as expensive here as it is in Paris. I'd like to sell a second film scenario . . . and I'm thinking actively about it.

My daughter is fine. The nurse reports that in all her behavior she has the air of a boy . . .

Georges Wague

Paris, early September 1917

. . . I'm leaving this evening for Limousin. You can write me at Castel-Novel, in Varetz, Corrèze. The ministerial crisis will doubtless recall Sidi, who will be remobilized, I'm afraid. Apart from that, I've spent the past three or four weeks extricating myself from a crisis—oh, quite ordinary—of poverty. We know this sort of thing, don't we? And while I was occupied with this crisis, I lost a manuscript in the Métro, a manuscript of which I hadn't a note or copy. Well, I'm not delicate, but that evening Sidi found me in bed, shivering, with a hot-water bottle at my feet, and a temperature of 80 degrees outside. The next morning I had "recovered" enough to harness myself to the most vomitory job I've ever faced in my life, beginning again on something already finished. Now it's done, and retyped.

You'll gather from this anecdote that I am working—in fact, doing nothing else. Soon I shall have the joy of publishing *Les Heures longues*, a book whose advance was devoted to furnishing Rozven back in 1914. *Plus ça change* . . .

André Billy*

Paris, mid-January 1918

Would you be inclined—or would your relationship with *L'Oeuvre* permit you—to contribute stories to *Le Matin*? I have been assigned to resurrect the old rubric *Mille et un Matins*, and I thought of you.

Have you received the extremely thin little volume I sent you?

* André Billy (1882–1971), veteran novelist, critic, and biographer who became a member of the Goncourt Academy only a few months before Colette was elected in 1945. His reviews of Colette's books were among the most perceptive she received.

Paris, end of January 1918

Can you tell me where this story of the "Rhone landscape"* comes from?

Les Heures longues hardly deserves the praise you accorded it, but I'm not complaining. How could I complain, moreover, when my husband has just arrived for a ten-day leave. All is fine. The Gros Chat is purring like a motor!

Georges Wague

Paris, mid-June 1918

I've have been spending painful days—and nights. Sidi has been at the most dangerous point of the offensive. He passed for dead or a prisoner, and conducted himself like a gallant, brave man throughout . . .

Francis Carco†

Paris, July 1918

Yes, I have received both *Les Innocents* and *Jésus-la-caille*. Tomorrow I'll send you *Les Heures longues*, which amounts only to slight journalistic squibs, I assure you. The only good thing is *La Chienne*. You were right to contact me. I have a feeling that we speak the same language. I have discovered *Les Innocents* and reread *Jésus-la-caille*. A beautiful, closed world, somber and simple, where three hundred words of argot suffice to express everything . . .

---

* In his review of *Les Heures longues*, Billy reported that, having fallen asleep on a train bound for the Midi, Colette was awakened by a companion, who urged her to admire the magnificence of the moonlight on the Rhone Valley. Colette opened one eye, groaned faintly, and went back to sleep. The next morning she had to write a story for a newspaper, and in two hours she produced a description of the moonlit river valley which, said Billy, "Chateaubriand would have envied had he known Colette." The same story was told later by Georges Wague, but the landscape was Lake Geneva.

† Francis Carco (1886–1958) wrote novels and poems celebrating the Paris of Montmartre nights, *apaches*, *bals-musettes*, and bad boys with soft hearts. He and Colette were close friends throughout her life.

What are you going to be doing down there? Live, I suppose, between the door and the bed in the window? Live, obviously, and work. I can do nothing. My husband has just spent five days here, having escaped from the worst fighting in Picardy. He behaved like a brave man, but was not wounded, alas. He has just left and I am trying to endure my inevitable cowardice. What a beautiful expression: "with an atrocious fervor," in your *Malheurs de Fernande*.

Paris, August 9, 1918

My husband has just spent eight days here, which explains your not hearing from me. Eight days . . . Yes, send me the manuscript of your novel for *L'Oeuvre*. With the help of Annie de Pène we'll place it with Téry. Meantime, for you, it's arthritis? Won't this perhaps mean your liberty? The liberty to work, and dine out in Montmartre, where the bombardments have been heavy? It's their turn. Auteuil had it regularly day before yesterday. But I'm coming to *Les Malheurs de Fernande*. Even with the first chapter, which I have not yet read, it's too short. But then, I'm sure that when you publish a volume of 600 pages, I'll be telling you: it's too short. I like your books. The rain, the little bistros, the strange bureaucracy of the prostitutes' lives, and their austere absence of fun—you are the present-day master of this literature . . .

Paris, early September 1918

. . . I have certainly received your letters. I'm getting used to them. There is such an agreeable warmth in a young friendship such as yours: I haven't the courage to give it up . . . It's 85 degrees in the shade, and my husband has liver trouble. He's been here for five days. When you leave Dax, will you pass through Paris? I hope so. We'll dine on La Butte, which I am told has been invaded by curious Americans. What travel agency can have sent them there? This isn't a letter. I only wanted to tell you that I have not yet received the manuscript and that I'll be happy to see you again.

Georges Wague

Castel-Novel, end of October 1918

I'm on agricultural leave with Sidi and my daughter, hence my silence. But all good things are soon over. We'll be returning Wednesday, and as soon as I'm back, I'll ask d'Estournelles de Constant for an interview. I want to settle this matter once and for all.

Yes, the Spanish flu . . . I'm going to miss Annie de Pène. What an imbecilic death! She neglected to have lunch or dinner, or perhaps skipped a meal to lose weight, and the flu caught her without defense, that is, with an empty stomach. Remember this, both of you.

My daughter is a love! What a film actress she'd make!

Francis Carco

Paris, February 24, 1919

I'm returning the review. It's what we call a rave. I had lunch with Alfred Savoir, who had just discovered *Jésus-la-caille* and was delirious about it. To keep his temperature high, I told him to dash out and buy *Les Innocents* at once. You must come here some evening for dinner and meet him. I'll see him again at the opening of *The Merchant of Venice*, and set a date.

As you can see, I'm still here. The British War Ministry has refused to allow civil air passengers to disembark on British soil. So we'll have to go by way of Strasbourg or Bordeaux or Marseilles . . .

Paris, end of February 1919

I received *Au coin des rues* this morning and read it on the spot. Truly, it contains twenty pages, perhaps more, that the best writer would envy. We'll talk about it when we meet chez Savoir on Wednesday . . . Tell me, is *Le Possédé* purely (or impurely) imaginary? If Jean Lorrain were living, he would be at your knees—if I may put it that way . . .

Maurice Ravel

Paris, March 1919

By all means, a ragtime! And Negroes in Wedgwood—certainly! And do let a terrifying gust from the Music Halls stir the dust at the Opéra!

I am pleased to know that you are still working on the *Divertissement pour ma fille.* * I had been told you were ill. Do you know that the cinema orchestras are playing your charming *Contes de ma Mère l'Oye* as background music for a Far West film? If I were a composer named Ravel, it seems to me I should be delighted to hear that.

Let the squirrel say whatever you wish. Did the "cat duet," entirely mee-e-owed, seem right? Are we to have acrobats? And will the arithmetic character dance a polka?

I trust you are in good health, and I clasp your hand— impatiently.

Roland Dorgelès†

Paris, early April 1919

I hadn't realized that *Les Croix de bois* was *your* book. It's magnificent. Jouvenel admires it even more than I, because he lived through it. I'm going to be ruthless about getting stories from you! At once, *at once*, do you hear me?—I want stories. We want to go out of town for Easter, and I need a backlog of good stories. I implore you to send me at least one *before* next Wednesday.

---

* The original title of Colette's libretto for the opera which became *L'Enfant et les sortilèges.*
† Roland Dorgelès (1886–19–?), who, said Colette, "never misses a chance to explode like a roasted chestnut," was another of the writers who celebrated the Paris of Montmartre and wound up their long careers in the Académie Goncourt.

Henry Bordeaux*

Paris, early April 1919

I am implacable. I want stories. We're leaving town on Easter and I need stories. I shall hector you as much as is necessary. And I have a creditor's soul . . .

Paris, April 1919

I'm desolate. Bataille's play had just finished, and I wanted to see all the copy, to be sure that it would appear, so I came around to the *Matin* office, only to be told you had been there and gone. I was crushed. You're on the Métro station at Ranelagh, I'm at Auteuil. Shall Auteuil come to Ranelagh? If I don't hear from you, I shall appear on Wednesday at three-thirty, and I shall not leave without a text.

Francis Carco

Paris, early April 1919

Two days ago, Sidi read the short story which you left with me, and yesterday he said: "Listen, he may very well be inaugurating a charming cycle of new stories here, but from the point of view of the *Matin* and Carco, publication would be a mistake. Carco has not yet appeared in a newspaper of large circulation, but for good reason he is already well known. If Carco were to offer us this story later on, it would be fine. But for his first appearance in the *Mille et un Matins*, he owes it to himself and to us to be represented by the sort of Carco story which the public already knows. It's up to him to give the *Matin* one or a series of *carçoises* stories. I don't say that this will be easy, I only say that this is what he should do. If you make him understand what I am telling you, he will understand that my decision is in his own best interests and that I am not merely thinking of the *Matin*."

* Henry Bordeaux (1870–1963), novelist, biographer, and member of the Académie Française.

I am summarizing what Sidi said, dear Carco, but on reflection, I think he is right. I am sure you can give us a Carco series, with Carco characters, Carco sensibilities, and the Carco milieu, of which, says Sidi, "you are at the present time the master painter." (The bugger doesn't hesitate to venture strong language, as you see. I should never dare use such unabashed terms.) But write me at once and let me know how you feel.

Otherwise, it's raining, on my gray boots and on my bulldog Gamelle. Still no coal at Rozven and the 14th is going to surprise me on a stage. Meantime, Jane Diris is in great pain. I've just come from her. She had consultations with important doctors yesterday, and further consultations are scheduled for today . . . It's a great pity, and I feel bitterly helpless before that splendid body which is ambushed by something invisible, energetic, and capricious.

Henry Bordeaux

Paris, early May 1919

Here I am, waiting for a story by Henry Bordeaux. I am sitting on the ground and weeping, when I am not cursing. All of this is very sad, and I ask you, with ultimate vehemence, to bring this state of things to a stop . . .

Henri Duvernois*

Rozven, summer 1919

I am even more scandalous than you would believe. I neither read, nor write, nor think. I spend my time clearing furze, carving a path along the hill, and digging out a ferocious undergrowth of brambles and thorns in a little pine wood that has been buried for years. I go swimming three times a day, I fish for shrimp and crabs, and on moonlight nights, for flounder and sole. I swim on my back, my stomach, my side,

* Henri Duvernois (1875–1937), novelist and playwright, specializing in lower-middle-class milieux.

all with the pride of a louse. I bark at strangers who use our private coast path as a shortcut. I watch my daughter and the movements of her beautiful little body. All this and nothing else! How can you live in Paris?

Francis Carco

Rozven, late August 1919

. . . Since the 25th of July, I have written only four letters, and two of those, I believe, were business letters. The rest of the time I swim, cut brush, fish, and loaf, above all, swim. Carco, this place is incomparable . . .

Your article on Modigliani is remarkable, my child. It is written with love, and in fine language, and it can disturb old, loitering people such as myself, for whom Modigliani has never proved very seductive . . . When will you be in Paris? I'm counting heavily on you to help console me for having to leave Rozven . . . Meantime, my play has turned into a novel, and I have forty-three written pages!!! I'll be in Paris September 15.

Hélène Picard*

Castel-Novel, 1919

I haven't the time to write you a real letter, since all I have to do is pick lilacs and wild orchids, ride horseback, watch my daughter, and light wood fires. But I am thinking of you, at least. Would you ever like to come here for a visit? You would have an immense room, a fireplace that looks lovely but doesn't give much heat, hoot owls, nightingales, sardonic magpies, fresh milk, and raw onions with every meal. The cat has had three kittens in a closet. Tomorrow we baptize the

---

* Hélène Picard (1873–1945), author of *Pour un mauvais garçon*, a collection of poems which Colette admired and frequently quoted. In the twenties she was Colette's secretary on *Le Matin*, after which she lived in aloof retirement in an apartment decorated in blue, tending her parakeets and writing poems. After Marguerite Moreno and Germaine Beaumont, she was perhaps Colette's dearest female friend. *L'Étoile vesper* contains an exceptionally tender portrait.

son of a farmer's wife and have bacon soup. Everything here would please you, I'm sure. The cider tastes divine and my daughter is the color of a ripe apple . . .

Castel-Novel, 1919

I am overrun by children, and all of the Jouvenel species. You know Bertrand and Colette, of course, but now there is a 12½-year-old boy, Renaud, who is terrible, seductive, wild, tender, destructive, and entirely astonishing. What force, already, in this infant Sidi! As for the grownup Sidi, I have only seen him one night. If he doesn't come back at once after the congress, I'll join him in Paris . . .

Léopold Marchand*

Castel-Novel, April 1920

Everything is too beautiful here. I'm drunk on it. And in addition my arm is trembling from having driven the tractor. Have you ever seen me on my tractor? The lilacs abound, pouring their scent onto the air. The nightingales have not yet learned their cavatina, but God knows they're rehearsing constantly! My daughter is a very agreeable sort of progressive peasant. She talks anatomy, circulatory system, pistil and stamen, and carbonic oxide. She knows the names of the four little bones in the ear, and it's high time, since I've forgotten them. Write me. Tell me everything, and above all don't be too polite . . .

Marguerite Moreno

Castel-Novel, April 4, 1920

I've been here ten days, and I'll be back in Paris on Saturday, or Sunday or Monday, depending on what train seats

---

* Léopold Marchand (1888–1952), author of some fifteen plays produced in Paris between 1919 and 1951, as well as Colette's collaborator in the stage adaptations of *Chéri* (1921) and *La Vagabonde* (1923). He and his wife, Misz, who committed suicide in 1942, were among Colette's most cherished friends.

are to be had. Apart from my daughter, who is ruddy, proud, bursting her seams, there is a family here which would delight you. Claire Boas nearly joined us, since in Paris we became old friends within twenty minutes. But she entrusted her charming son to me, and Mamita has come down too. Sidi hovers over us all, with a Mohammedan serenity . . .

Hélène Picard

Castel-Novel, early June 1920
. . . I have been working desperately hard at *Chéri* since yesterday. It must not only be finished but polished . . .

Castel-Novel, June 1920
Just think—*Chéri* is finished! I can't get over it, and Sidi liked it when I read it to him. You will see how I celebrated my deliverance when you see my hands and arms. I'm simply one large wound—though an enchanted one—from battling with rosebushes and nettles.

Lucie Saglio

Paris, June 12, 1920
You're a fine fellow and a perfect friend, and I regret not coming to your house this evening. I should certainly come if I could be sure of not encountering Saglio at your table. I have just received a letter in which he refuses to pay me the price he promised me for serializing *Chéri* in *La Vie Parisienne*. Having added fifteen hundred francs to the original five thousand francs he had already given me, he considers himself paid up. Now (and Marcel Prévost reproached me bitterly for doing so) I only gave *Chéri* to Saglio because he boasted that he would pay me "better than anyone else." I should be satisfied if he merely paid me *as well as anyone else.* But I cannot tolerate these slave trader's tactics and I shall "drop" Charles Saglio.

Losing money is less important than losing a friend. I

don't want to lose you. Please assure me that we shall remain friends and let's get together wherever you wish, *chez moi*, for instance. In any case, I remain very affectionately attached to you, and I hug you with all my heart.

P.S. Now listen! I know you . . . Don't try to "arrange the matter" personally. Saglio cannot redeem himself with a mere check. Let's leave it at that, please?

Marcel Proust

Paris, June 1920

Cher ami, how are you? I have not acknowledged your letter at once but I think of you very often. They are still printing and binding *Chéri*, but I am uneasy as to your opinion, and in my impatience, I am sending you a set of proofs. They are not corrected, but never mind. *Chéri* is a sort of novel I have never written before. My others—the "vagabondes" and "entraves"—were more or less extensions of the *Claudines*. If only I were lucky enough to have a new Marcel Proust for my vacation—that and the sea!

Hélène Picard

Rozven, July 1920

Your room is waiting for you. Hurry up with your autographing books and let me know the hour you'll be arriving, so I can have Jean meet you at the station. Would you also be kind enough to bring me the story Sapène rejected? It's called "L'Habitude."* Either the ms. or the proof must be in the middle drawer of my desk.

The weather is glorious, pure Rozven weather. Léo has caught a huge octopus . . . Yesterday he was reading aloud from *Province et capucines* with a fervor which would have touched you, and Misz had tears in her eyes . . .

---

* Included in a 1924 collection of short stories called *La Femme cachée*, "L'Habitude" was probably rejected by *Le Matin*'s conservative editor because it described the breaking up of a lesbian ménage.

Francis Carco

Rozven, early July 1920

... How does a collective arrival Monday morning strike you? Telephone Germaine and Hélène and then telegraph me. The evening train leaves the Gare des Invalides at 9:50. You can reserve sleepers. Bring *sweaters*, swimsuits, and rope-soled sandals, which are the only ones that don't slip on the rocks. If you have a bathrobe or two, bring them for your own use—I have no extras. Tell Germaine that city hats are not worn here. Any straw hat will do—I have plenty. I can think of nothing else to tell you except that I'll be ravished to see you . . .

Rozven, early September 1920

... a quick bulletin:

Bel-Gazou is at Castel-Novel.

Hélène has not yet left for Toulouse, and she's crazy about you. Write to her!

Sidi is harassed but ready to leave for Limousin.

Meg is exhausted and doesn't look good. Her health should be watched over. When a woman is earning money, has pretty dresses, a man in her bed, another man pleading to get into her bed, a third man—moreover, a good-looking and enamored gigolo—clamoring for the same privilege— and this same woman is sad and sallow—watch out for her liver!

. . . *Chéri* in its fifty-third thousand? What do you mean? Thirty-first thousand is more like it. But if it continues to sell we hope for a reprinting in November . . .

Paris, early October 1920

Cher Carco, what a week*—of congratulations, openings, red ribbons, thises and thats! When I realize that I have not yet written you, I'm ashamed. I've been wined and dined,

---

* Colette had been named Chevalier de la Légion d'Honneur on September 25.

Marchand follows in my footsteps, Sapène gave me a dinner, Sarah Bernhardt sent me a telegram. At Castel-Novel, Sidi and his three offspring organized a parade, requisitioning all the armor and ghosts in the house, the children even tied my writing materials in red ribbon—and you weren't there!

Jean de Pierrefeu*

Paris, mid-October 1920

But what are you up to, dear Pierrefeu and others, in trying to regenerate me? Léa, and Chéri even more so, are indeed poor creatures, but is it so vile to write about them? It seems to me that I have written nothing so moral as *Chéri*. Raise your eyebrows in desperation, but all the same shake my hand affectionately. For I regard you highly and I do thank you for the beautiful review . . .

Comtesse Anna de Noailles

Paris, autumn 1920

Thank you for having sent me *Les Forces éternelles*. It perhaps occurred to you that no one would admire your book more than I. Every time, whether by accident or inclination, I open one of your books, I get absorbed and lost in it. It's hard to escape you . . . Jouvenel is as taken with you as I am, but he is better at expressing just how much and why. I shall send you *Chéri* if you wish, though I am afraid you won't like it. It's a novel about sad people, almost unworthy of suffering.

Charles Saglio

Paris, late December 1920

A cup of blue crystal, some very good chocolates, and your card.

---

* Jean de Pierrefeu (1891–1940), critic, journalist, and one of Colette's most alert readers from 1913 on. The review of *Chéri* to which Colette refers was very severe, concluding: "Her art portrays strange milieux, vulgar and without interest, which nevertheless Colette seems to delight in . . . She has too much genius to go on degrading it in this manner."

But listen, Charles Saglio, you caused me a great deal of pain, and even wrath, this past year. Is all that over now? Are you worth so much torment? I don't know. I am probably being a fool—but I am also affectionate.

Léopold Marchand

Castel-Novel, May 5, 1921

Well now, my child, the play is finally finished. Yesterday evening I read the third act to Sidi and I must say that he was very moved. I had rewritten the end of the third act three times, cursing and swearing . . . I suppressed the filmic effect of silence. And Chéri does all the talking! It will be easy to play. I leave for Paris Sunday evening. Make an appointment with Silvestre for Tuesday or Wednesday or Thursday . . . As for my daughter, she is now planning to marry, have seven children, and put them all to work. The four boys will do the farming. One daughter will sweep, another sew, and the third do the cooking. "They needn't expect me to spoil them!" . . . I'm still prowling through the *Goncourt Journal*, since I don't want to read anything distracting. Do you know what Maupassant said about England? "Too many toothbrushes and not enough bidets!"

Lucie Saglio

Paris, June 2, 1921

I'm about to leave for the opening night of Rothschild's new play, and I have just had time to pin two of your roses to my belt. You are a love, a sensitive, and nervous, and vulnerable love. I am sorry if *Chéri* made you weep. Permit his author to hug you tight.

Marcel Proust

Paris, early July 1921

Cher ami, if instead of writing reviews, attending banquets in Limousin, and reading manuscripts for *Le Matin,* I led a life of leisure—and oh how well I know what such a life of leisure would consist of: the luxury of not hurrying, and

I would ride about in an old-fashioned victoria!—I should have long since given myself the pleasure of writing to you about your new book. If I were to tell you that I burrow in its pages every night before going to sleep, you would think I was merely offering you a hollow compliment. But the fact is, Jouvenel gets into bed every night to find me, your book, and my glasses. "I am jealous but resigned," he says. The beginning of *Sodom* dazzled him. No one—but no one in the world—has ever written comparable pages on inversion! Years ago I wanted to write a study of sexual inversion myself, and it was the substance of your pages that I wanted to express. But my laziness or incapacity failed to get it down . . . I swear that after you, apart from yourself, no one will be able to add anything to what you have written. Who, after you, would dare to touch the lepidopterous, vegetal, birdlike watchfulness of a Jupien at the approach of a Charlus? It's all magnificent—and then the portrait of the Princesse de Parme! How I do admire you, and how eagerly I wish you good health and happiness . . .

Léopold Marchand

Rozven, July 1921

. . . Don't count on my writing you a long letter, full of ingenious perceptions and definitive sentences on the conjugal life awaiting you. If I were to write such a letter, it might tempt you to stay on in Paris instead of coming here where you'll have the sea, sun, and sand, the incessant breathing of the waves, cider, warm nights, cool days, striped cats, three amiable children—and me. So come. Do you happen to have boxing gloves? And don't forget to bring rope-soled sandals. The coast is hot and fragrant. In the evening, a rosary of lighthouses gleam along the bays . . .

Marguerite Moreno

Rozven, early August 1921

. . . In one month and five days, I'll be back in Paris, and I shall come to see you in *Le Chemineau*. Meantime, you are sweet to like *Chéri.* I know nothing about him, though they tell me he is selling . . .

Hélène Picard

Rozven, mid-August 1921

Your story "Le Larcin" is charming . . . I allowed myself to cut the words *Eau de Lubin*, which constitute a plug for a product and would bring Sapène down on our necks. I have also questioned *concupiscence*, which will make the retired cop in Rueil sit up and growl. Finally I have spelled *ylang-ylang* with a *g*, instead of a *d*, because that's the correct spelling. So. Having played schoolmistress, I'll shut up . . .

Marguerite Moreno

Rozven, August 17, 1921

. . . Nothing and no one is more obstinately set against work at this moment than I am. I have written a few short stories, but now I am dry, peevish at the sight of blank paper, and although Léo keeps cutting up and rearranging the script of *La Vagabonde* into a distinguished mosaic, I only respond with groans and blasphemies. . . . I must not forget to tell you that Roulette is bursting at the seams, thanks to the handsome little Belgian griffon she was married to last June. If all goes well, I shall have a splendid litter. She's due to give birth about the 5th of September, and she already looks like a little sow.

Castel-Novel, September 22, 1921

. . . The house is comfortable, well supplied with flies, and the children are superb—Bertrand follows me about like a dog . . . Sidi is getting better, thanks to large doses of quinine and milk. The two little griffon pups would drive you crazy. Think of me, wait for me, I'll come to your theater as soon as I'm back. Are you happy with your Mélisande of the Fortifications? I urge you to make do with passing temptations. What can one be sure of if not what one holds in one's arms at the time one is holding it? And we have so few chances to be proprietary . . . I do love you, always, and I doubt if we shall ever change the nature of our "friendship" for each other . . .

Hélène Picard

Castel-Novel, January 1, 1922

It's the first of January, so I'm thinking of you. I can also smell garlic, sausage, and cream cheese mixed with pepper and raw onion. My children are behaving very nicely, so I'm letting myself live a little, though at the same time I'm working. Yesterday evening we ate pine nuts, popping the cones into the fire to snap and crackle. This morning Colette and I gathered holly. It's a pure life, with hoot owls wandering in the freezing hallways! But I must bring you here. The attics and ghosts would inspire a thousand stories.

Léopold Marchand

Castel-Novel, January 2, 1922

. . . By sweating blood, I have just managed to finish a story, and a little copy for the *Revue de Paris*. Don't talk to me about *Le Disparu*. It was acceptably cut at the beginning, but then strangely punctuated with asterisks, and the result was shabby . . .

Paris, February 22, 1922

My child—I have finally had to send you a telegram, since every time I sat down to write you a letter someone came into the room, or the telephone rang, or some other nuisance came up. When your own letter arrived, I sniffed it, read both sides of the paper, and shook it like a carpet slipper. Then, holding it in my mouth and walking on my hind legs, I took it in to Sidi. He considered it for a long moment— four seconds—and said: "But this idiot, this bandy-legged skunk, this bum—*is absolutely right.*" As you see, I entirely agree with him. So get on with it! You're pure theater, and wonderful, and oh so very young . . .

Paris, March 7, 1922

Don't be irritated or uneasy. You know I'm doing a thousand things, and that every time "I'm going to write Léo," something or someone interferes. For instance: in a taxi I lost my bag, along with thirty pages of my next novel—and not a line of any other version!—as well as this week's story for *Le Matin*, and a hundred miscellaneous papers. I've been haunting the Lost and Found bureau and tomorrow I'll run a notice in the paper. But it's poisoned me. And then I spent half a day with an American lady who wants to film *Chéri*. And then Rasimerde wants me to give a little talk at every performance of the road company *Chéri*—otherwise, he claims, no money. And Moreno's mother died, murmuring, "I'd gladly eat a biscuit . . ." And the dentist! But at least I have a pretty new tooth . . .

Marguerite Moreno

Paris, May 12, 1922

Did you read in *Le Matin* that a certain lady of letters miraculously escaped death when her car was reduced to pulp by a truck? That lady was me. The car is in pieces and the fact that I emerged unhurt, albeit crawling, is amazing . . . All goes well here. My daughter is pink and sharp-witted. Sidi is fat. But at Castel-Novel I weighed myself: almost 81 kilos!!!

Léopold Marchand

Rozven, July 12, 1922

Come whenever you wish or are able, *mon petit Léo*. And bring the copy of *La Vagabonde*, which naturally I forgot. I'll be very happy to see you. I was more worn out than I suspected. I can measure my diminution by the difference between myself this year and myself in the year past . . . Just imagine that in an entire week I haven't yet ventured so much as a swim, or even a walk. I'm an old woman! Where's my lorgnette . . .

Marguerite Moreno

Rozven, July 16, 1922

It's still cold here. Each day contains samples of all four seasons, and all the varieties of "weather." Rain-whipped mornings, very mild mornings, beautiful afternoons, with northwest wind, sometimes freezing, sometimes warm evenings. We're still waiting for the "perfect July heat." I'm feeling better, but my progress is very slow. The temperature of the sea does not permit me to swim, so Bel-Gazou and I splash together . . .

Rozven, August 1, 1922

. . . I need a note from you. I'm becoming uneasy. Besides I'm still not completely cured. Oh, the human body—so quickly mortified . . . But I'm working. I'm trying to get up a backlog of stories for *Le Matin*. Sidi has already left, after eighteen days of vacation. As a "souvenir of the Emerald Coast," he is bringing back a "whiplash" in the right calf . . . So now I'm alone, with Bel-Gazou and Bertrand, my great greyhound of a stepson, who is beginning to look like a country boy. As for my daughter . . . she is abominable. She roots out onions in the garden and eats them. She hides in the attic and plays hopscotch with the maid. But a mother's life is ever a tribulation, as Madame Peloux would say.

Lucie Delarue-Mardrus

Rozven, 1922

. . . You're living entirely alone these days? That's fine. But now that I am no longer young I am afraid of solitude, besides which I have become used to being with children . . .

Léopold Marchand

Paris, September 23, 1922

I'm dashing this letter off in telegraphese. Yes, have the big scene typed. As for the fourth-act décor, I'd prefer a Marseilles bistro to anything so flossy as the Réserve. I don't know who should play Brague or Laissé-pour-compte.

I'm working on the first act. The first two acts of Brieux's new play are good—at least they seemed so at the dress rehearsal. But the third act is shoddy and predictable. And then the characters are constantly *telling* us what happens instead of making it happen. As for Falconetti—she's a fraud. No makeup and unbelievably *old* hair—she thinks she's another Duse . . . I hope she croaks. She's now asking a thousand francs for a rehearsal, because she won three thousand francs at the gambling table one evening at Deauville . . . Moreover, she is not so overwhelming as an actress. Too much pent-up emotion. Tears, tears, tears. And frenetic pawing of the face to assure the public that she's not wearing makeup!

Pierre Blanchar*

Paris, December 27, 1922

But "Rêverie de nouvel an" is an old thing! I was a young woman when I wrote it, and a young woman can always teach her elders how to grow old. Later on, she stops to consider the matter, and finds she has forgotten the lesson she once taught herself . . .

Hélène Picard

Lyons, early 1923

. . . what a life! Tomorrow I leave again and spend yet another night on the train. But this morning at least I can play lazybones and stay in bed. It's been a long time since I've seen you, but you know without my demonstrating it how tenderly I love you, and what carefully concealed respect I feel for your genius and for your great virtues as a loner. But neither of us is temperamentally inclined to brandish our affections. When I get back to Paris, you will have finished *Sabbat*—and then we'll raise our glasses to your good health!

---

* Pierre Blanchar (1896–1963), an actor distinguished for his performances, on stage, in *La Prisonnière* and *L'Idiot*, and, on the screen, in *La Symphonie pastorale.* "New Year's Reverie," an autobiographical sketch, is included in *Earthly Paradise.*

Marguerite Moreno

Paris, April 10, 1923

. . . Just imagine that I arrived home—intending to lunch alone—and I opened the drawer of my little desk to get some money—and a single letter fell out, a letter from my mother, written in pencil, one of her last, with unfinished words and an implicit sense of her departure . . . It's so curious: one can resist tears and "behave" very well in the hardest hours of grief. But then someone makes you a friendly sign behind a window—or one notices that a flower that was in bud only yesterday has suddenly blossomed, or a letter slips from a drawer—and everything collapses.

Hélène Picard

Castel-Novel, spring 1923

. . . If only you could see the persimmon tree, laden with half-ripe fruit! It's a marvel, like something from the Blessed Isles. And the violets! . . . Sidi is no longer here. But I gather he has been gone a week, returning to Paris and then leaving again. Isn't youth wonderful?

Castel-Novel, May 1923

. . . Everything is fine but the weather, which is torrential. Today we were able to go out, but yesterday! In spite of which, the nightingales and the roses are flourishing, and even the strawberries are coming along. But what roses! They cover everything—the house, the walls, the gardens . . . The more I cut, the more there are . . .

Marguerite Moreno

Castel-Novel, June 1923

I've finished—or I think I've finished—*Le Seuil.** But not without torment! The last page, precisely, cost me my entire first day here—and I defy you, when you read it, to suspect this. Alas, that a mere twenty lines, without fancy effects or

* Published in July 1923, as *Le Blé en herbe.*

embossing of any kind, should make such demands. It's the *proportions* that give me the greatest trouble. And I have such a horror of grandiloquent finales . . .

Your letter made me happy just because you wrote it. I'm planning a visit to your apartment. I'll arrive at an improbable hour, carrying my 175 pounds and my air of false assurance, along with cigarettes, some of those Spanish honey-and-almond cakes, a liter of port, Bertrand, Pati-Pati—in other words, my usual cortege of material provisions . . .

A battalion of nightingales is singing in the rain. It doesn't bother them in the least. One in particular, very near the house, sings day and night with a cold sheen, a pure, charmless virtuosity which would leave even the most romantic of virgins—for instance, our Hélène—untroubled . . .

Hélène Picard

Rozven, summer 1923

. . . We arrived yesterday to find Rozven radiant, sizzling hot, and abounding with toads as large as my behind. The sea seemed cold at first, but got warmer, and the sand heals all blights, moral and physical alike . . .

Paris, September 29, 1923

. . . I'll send you a *pneumatique* Monday so you'll know if the *Masque de fer* opening is still that night. Meantime, I've just finished my daily stint—a review of Verneuil's *La Maîtresse de bridge*. It's a pitiful play. I've never felt so smothered or sat through such gloomy gaiety. And just think—it's Verneuil who is the director of the Renaissance Theater and who wants to stage a revival of *La Vagabonde!* Life can be complicated . . .

Paris, October 2, 1923

. . . My silence must have puzzled you. It's because Sidi came home. It's because, on the way back from picking up

Bel-Gazou in Fontainebleau, the car broke down twice. (I had a dinner engagement in Paris and at seven-thirty I was still somewhere in the dust, beyond the fortifications, en route.) It's because I escorted Bel-Gazou to her jail in Saint-Germain, and the "entrance formalities" left me half out of my head, with fifteen minutes for dinner before going on to Maurice Rostand's longest and flimsiest and worst play. We emerged at 1:30 a.m., and I am writing you this before getting down—alas—to my review. I won't be at *Le Matin* today, except to correct my proof . . . but later I'll bring you some roses . . .

Léopold Marchand

Castel-Novel, October 19, 1923

. . . Yes, do come. But in heaven's name bring some flyswatters. It won't last, but for the moment it's like midsummer here. The flies think it's July and behave accordingly.

. . . God knows where Sidi is. He was to have arrived here before us, but I haven't heard a word from him. Meantime, his mail is being naïvely forwarded from Paris, revealing that he himself left town the day after I did . . .

Hélène Picard

Castel-Novel, October 1923

I should be writing you every day if it weren't for this damned lecture I'm preparing . . . It's exasperating, but otherwise life would be extremely agreeable, because the weather is beautiful almost every day, with a warmth so imperious and so gentle that it seems a form of grace. Of course, having to work spoils it all. Your letter has given me great pleasure, since you're getting better. Unhappily I won't be the one who drives you to the clinic. The car won't be returning to Paris. It's being repaired at Brive and I'll pick it up on my lecture route, which takes me to a city per day for eight days: Nice, Toulon, Marseilles, Aix, Avignon,

Lyons, etc. Without the car, I would have to manage my baggage and catch trains alone, and at all hours of the day and night, which would leave me worn out . . .

Marguerite Moreno

Castel-Novel, October 20, 1923

. . . I'll be in Paris in ten days, perhaps sooner. Sidi will be there Sunday morning . . . We're having a burning south wind, with brusque showers, but how good the sun feels! Work is poisoning my life. Having painfully begotten thirty pages of my lecture on "The problem of life *à deux*," I have realized that for the moment, and for many reasons, I must leave this subject alone. So I've renounced it and begun "What I have seen from the stage in the audience, and from the audience on the stage," or something of that sort. But what a lot of time wasted!

Castel-Novel, October 1923

. . . a travel bulletin to keep you up to date. It was a long trip, due to the road conditions, not to mention the condition of Jean's* derriere. The poor fellow arrived half dead with pain from an abscess in the anus—can you imagine? I had him operated on at once and now he's recovering very well. Then, after twelve hours of getting settled here, Pauline was called to the bedside of her dying mother . . . Sidi has not yet appeared, though his mail tells me that he left Paris on our heels . . . Amour, amour . . . Anagram of amour: rouma. Add "nia" and you find a lady† who has the bones of a horse and hatches books in two volumes. Our Sidi has no luck . . . I expect him from hour to hour, day to day, week to week . . .

* Colette's chauffeur.
† Colette is apparently inferring that Sidi's current romantic interest was a Roumanian novelist, Princesse Marthe Bibesco.

Hélène Picard

Bordeaux, November 1923

Bonjour, mon Hélène. I arrive, depart, arrive again, depart again. And I'm being a very good girl, I assure you! Last night I dreamed that you were completely cured, and that you came on foot to see me in a house in Passy with an interior courtyard. There were also dogs and two young friends with a newborn infant as large as a hand and *amphibious!* They put him in a basin and he swam with his head underwater like a fish. You see what I've come to!

Madame Léopold Marchand

Marseilles, November 23, 1923

I'll telephone you Sunday when I'll be back in Paris, with a thousand things to tell you. It's very tiring to change cities every day when one is traveling alone. Packing one's valise, checking one's purse, putting on and removing one's makeup . . . oufa! Otherwise, the tour has gone very well and I modestly acknowledge my success. I also acknowledge that I have never been so cold on unheated stages. But all this is banal. It's just that so much fuss and coming and going leaves little time to write to those one loves. The weather is bright, cold and sharp, and the mistral is no doubt a healthy form of ventilation but a rude one. It's rampant at this very moment.

Marguerite Moreno

Bordeaux, December 16, 1923

. . . Around and around I go. Bordeaux has covered me with flowers—literally. Sleeping cars enable me to catch up on the sleep I too often lose in Paris . . . Tomorrow I leave for Saint-Sebastien, where I speak on Monday. Tuesday I'm in Bayonne, and Wednesday I'm coming home. Bordeaux is a very handsome city, full of guzzling and feasting. I am introduced as *Mademoiselle* Colette de Jouvenel. It's one way of satisfying everyone . . .

Madame Georges Wague

Paris, January 6, 1924

But, my child, haven't you heard the gossip? We're in the same boat. If it is true that happiness is only relative, then think of yourself as happy, in comparison to me . . . You don't have a child, which is a pity—or work to absorb you. But come and see me, not at *Le Matin*, though, and not before next week. Telephone me Tuesday or Wednesday morning. And, *above all*, arrange to move, to get out of the house where you've been tormented. Find another nest. I know that's hard, but find one all the same, and at once. I am sure I am giving you good advice . . .

As for me, I've been alone for a month. He left without a word while I was on a lecture tour. I am divorcing.

Hélène Picard

Paris, January 12, 1924

. . . My silence and my absence must seem incomprehensible to you. Believe me, I have been working from 8:30 a.m. until one in the morning. I can't do more than that. Today, Saturday, I was at my worktable at 8:30, to produce eleven pages of a scenario which I left with Léo, Madame Sylvie, and Fauré. There followed lunch and two hours of exhausting palaver. At three, I was in the office of Mouthon, who directs the *Journal*. He is planning a weekly and wanted to discuss my writing for it. Two hours of palaver and figures with Vautel, Pawlowski, Henri Béraud, etc. At five I was on the Left Bank in the offices of Armand Colin, to whom I had sent the results of half a night's work. They were enchanted and things look good, but the project must be delivered by July at the latest. At 6:30 I was at the Maison de Blanc to be fitted for a snowsuit. At seven I was at *Le Matin* to deliver my next *Journal de Colette* column, written yesterday evening between 10:30 and 1 a.m. For the present, all my days are like this. Tomorrow, Sunday, I must be at the hairdresser's from two to six. At seven—if you please, oh, my Hélène

—two ministers, Klotz and Bérard, are picking me up and we are dining in Seine-et-Oise chez Mouthon with the other director of the *Journal*, and you can guess the extent to which this interests me. Then Monday morning at nine, I go to the dentist for a bitch of a molar which has been tormenting me since yesterday. In between now and then I must pack my bags—naturally, at night. Which means, my Hélène, that if I do not see you before I go, it will be my loss. I leave at eight. My address will be Hôtel Royal, Gstaad, Switzerland . . .

Marguerite Moreno

Gstaad, January 22, 1924

. . . Don't chide me for writing you so little and so late. From the moment I arrived here, I have had the urge to live physically with great intensity. I had my first ski lesson at once and since then I have been skating and tobogganing as well. I don't miss a chance to fall! They find me on the neighboring slopes, on my back like a scarab, waving my rear paws tangled in the skis. Passers-by stop, pick me up, and I go again. When Bertrand accompanies me—he skis very well and goes on guided runs—he looks after me. Otherwise, I spill out of the toboggan on the curves and find it all charming. Of course this is chiefly—oh, miracle!—because I have finally found a place where it's warm in the wintertime! The sun is baking. The sky is a brutal blue. There is an incomparable absence of wind. The South of France has never given me this! I swear I'll come back here—or to some other snowbound place. And there's a hotel where you can wear a jumper in your room, and a low-cut dress in the evening, without fearing the cold! These Swiss buggers run their hotels with a simplicity and comfort that put the Riviera palaces to shame. Of course there isn't a shred of taste or elegance—no pink lampshades or pretty cretonne covers—but boiling water and warm air flow everywhere. And what a table . . . You see how happy I am. I shall come

back broke but in a wonderful humor and with a sun-
tanned nose.

Hélène Picard

Don't hold it against me if I haven't yet been to see you!
I arrived at five this morning and found so many matters
to arrange, fight over, and protect myself against, that I've
had no time for anything else. Today I speak at the *Annales*,
after which I have an appointment with a publisher for new
editions of *Sept dialogues de bêtes* and *La Retraite sentimentale*. Meantime, I love you, I embrace you, and I hope to
see you soon looking like a freshly emerged butterfly . . .

I'll be in Switzerland when this reaches you. Please believe
me: I have simply not been *able* to see you. There was
one day when I might have managed it, but that was a day
when life seemed like so many broken reeds and I didn't
want to see anyone. I know how impressionable you are, and
my own bafflement would have overwhelmed you. I am tartly
inclined to regard my state as transitory, but all the same, I
had to stay in bed for twenty-four hours. The warmth and
immobility restored me and the next morning I returned
to my battle stations.

Meanwhile, let me report that arrangements with the
Journal are settled. I am to give them page-one copy twice
a week, one story per month, and the serial rights to my
next novel. What I must do now is secure my footing in
this new location and try to make myself esteemed. At the
same time, I must give some thought to a weekly piece for
a new magazine Mouthon is starting . . .

Blanche Vogt tells me that she is no longer on the staff of
L'Oeuvre! She seemed extremely worried and uneasy about
the future. Ah! la la, and again la la! We are an innumerable
lot of women, all tormented by the thought of tomorrow.

My little Hélène, is there something you need? If so, to whom can you appeal frankly if not your friend who embraces you tenderly?

Marguerite Moreno

Montreux, February 23, 1924

I have your letter, and I'm answering it hastily, as you know how eager I am that this *Rampe* become a source of income for you. You must not spoil your debut, which is why I am a bit perplexed when you speak of writing a piece about winter sports. Even if you hurry, your piece would be in the April issue at the earliest, wouldn't it? And wouldn't that be terribly out of season? . . . The time for a winter-sports piece is December, or January at the latest . . . You haven't told me enough for me to be of much help, but if your plans are made, and your first assignment brings you here—well, that would be grand . . .

I was as sick as a dog. My troubles had poisoned me. Here I'm feeling better already, riding a bobsled down the slope at seventy kilometers an hour . . .

Francis Carco

Montreux, early March 1924

. . . I was planning to return the 7th, but now I can stay until the 14th. The snow is still magnificent, and when you come here next year, you will see how deeply this cushion will winnow you, will wear you out—in the good sense—will massage and renew you. I came here to work on a novel, but naturally I've harnessed myself to something else. My progress is slight and difficult, but it is progress. All the same, it's terrible to think, as I do every time I begin a book, that I no longer have any talent, that in fact I never had any. Do you ever feel that way? But of course you're young . . .

Bertrand is fine. Apart from skiing and bobsledding, he finds perverse distraction in writing "some" books. His second political volume is almost finished. It amounts to a little lark in twenty chapters called *Victoire sans paix*. Being twenty years old has its neuroses.

. . . It's now seven-thirty—in the morning. It snowed again last night and the pines are all plumed in white. Clouds sail by under my nose, like giant fish . . .

Léopold Marchand

Brussels, April 12, 1924

. . . I saw M. de Jouvenel when I was in Paris. It appears that he will have his Ministry at last (!!!). Oufa! And moreover, he is going to give me a little car . . . The next day I ordered a Renault representative to call and when I get back to Paris I shall learn to drive! . . . It's tiresome of me to talk only about myself all the time. Here it's snowing, but there is enough rain mixed in to give an agreeable promise of spring.

Hélène Picard

Paris, April 29, 1924

. . . I'm sending you a copy of my first column in *Figaro*, but there's only one reason I am eager for you to read it: your name embellishes the last line. I embrace you with all my heart.

Maurice Ravel

Rozven, summer 1924

Oh! cher ami, when, when are we to have the *Divertissement pour ma fille*? Is it true that it's almost finished?

With hope and friendship.

Marguerite Moreno

Paris, July 2, 1924

It is eleven o'clock Wednesday morning, and I have just learned that Robert* died at 2 a.m. I've sent a note, which

* Robert de Jouvenel was Henry's brother.

doubtless will be ignored. Bertrand must be on the train coming back from Lyons. That's all I know about this sad story, except this: for days and nights the elder brother has been at Robert's bedside, refusing to leave him for a moment. It was—alas—the *only* great and deep affection of his life. I have also sent a note to Zou, and otherwise shall stay here . . . But poor Zou! What will she do, and especially what will she do with herself?

I saw Monzie yesterday. His faithful secretary told me that the day before yesterday he told her: "I have the impression that Henry regrets having upset his life with the separation . . ."

. . . Write me . . . I'm shaky and obsessed at the moment. Only half an hour ago I "sensed" something was wrong and I telephoned the hospital to find out what had happened. But the night before last I was awakened by a cry, not very loud, and uttered at my side by Jouvenel. The impression was so strong, and I am so little accustomed to such phenomena, that I turned on my lamp, drank some water, and checked on the time. It was just *two o'clock.* I never wake up at that time—always between four-thirty and five. This won't surprise you, of course. But for the past twenty-four hours I have lived with a constant palpitation . . .

Paris, July 10, 1924

. . . Bertrand has just returned from a frightful funeral at Castel-Novel . . . While there, his father had a compassionate word for him: "Take care of your health, above all . . . I don't want you to be unhappy . . ."

Meantime, my daughter has been in the school infirmary again for eight days. The staff told me she can be moved Saturday. "Take her to the seashore. She needs it, as she is passing through a period of growth and imbalance . . ." So what else can I do? We're going to Rozven and Bertrand will follow. But there's more! Léo and Misz Marchand are going on ahead. For family reasons they must be in Poland by August 25 at the latest. In the interim, Léo and I must finish two acts of our "new play" (we tell people that three acts are done already, but we're lying, of course) . . .

Rozven, July 26, 1924

Don't be uneasy, my dear soul. The trip went off without problems or breakdown and took three days. We've been here since Tuesday evening, with high winds. And Bertrand has no more temperature and my daughter is superb and both of them are eating like grasshoppers.

How I love your letters. Don't forget me. We'll end up together one day, you'll see. The change of air has been magnificent for Colette. Her cough vanished instantly. This isn't a real letter, only a health bulletin. I had such a horror of my fountain pen this week that I wired *Figaro*: "Ill. Article* will appear next week."

Rozven, August 12, 1924

. . . Now the heat has arrived, which would suffice to explain my silence to anyone but you. That imbecile Bertrand has been in Paris for eight days. He is organizing some democratic youth group or other daydream, and is due back the 15th . . . As for me, I work badly and swim very well, and the Léos are so sweet that their departure tomorrow breaks my heart . . . A missionary from Cameroon has sent me a silver bracelet which once adorned the dark wrist of a cannibal chief's favorite. The bracelet is handsome and heavy, a torsade of solid silver which attests the fineness of the wrist that wore it.

---

* From April 29 through October 5—with the exception of the week of July 26—Colette contributed a Sunday article to *Le Figaro*, under the heading "A Woman's Opinion." When her collaboration ceased, the twenty-two pieces were published as a book called *Aventures quotidiennes*, the title being chosen to make clear that Colette's loyalty as well as her by-line had now moved to a newspaper called *Le Quotidien*.

. . . Would you like to play Madame Peloux in Monte Carlo for three days next December? I'm asked to play Léa, and Léo would play the boxer Patron. If it works out, we could do other towns. Tell me what you think. I've said yes for Léo and myself. We certainly wouldn't be bored.

I'm collapsing with fatigue. Today we drove one hundred and twenty kilometers under the sun. Lunch at Pontaubault . . . at an inn which served us *eleven* dishes at nine francs apiece.

I love you with all my heart, idiot; now I'm off to bed . . .

Rozven, August 30, 1924

. . . I have had to write three columns in the past few days, and I assure you that I could have as easily given birth to triplets. And in addition, there's been correspondence, telegraphic and otherwise, with the *Quotidien*, where they're haggling. I am accepting 42,000 instead of 60,000—naturally, though, they say they will raise it soon. On the other hand, the 2,000-a-month francs for theater criticism will only be paid me during the drama season. I can't argue about that. *Le Matin* paid much worse. Let's not talk about it . . .

Léopold Marchand

Paris, September 8, 1924

. . . I'll be going back to Rozven this evening and expect you there. I haven't wasted my time here and think I'm going to make very good arrangements with the *Quotidien* . . . Now listen: we're making up a company of writers who can act. The publicity should be novel and amusing. What would you think of this cast:

Moreno—Madame Peloux
Dehon—Naronne de la Berche
Jeanne Landre—Aldonza *and* Rose
Germaine Beaumont—Poussier

Claude Chauvière—Chambermaid in Act II
Léo—Patron
And then a well-built young litterateur to play Desmond.
There are plenty around.

The Touring Writers' Company—it would work. And you
know, writers would cost much less than professional actors.

Marguerite Moreno

Rozven, mid-September 1924

. . . I should like to talk earnestly to you about your copy
for *Les Annales.* You still do not have quite the right touch.
You lack the seeming carelessness which gives the "diary"
effect. For the most part you have approached your gentle-
men as though they were so many subjects assigned in class
. . . For one portrait which works—Jarry—there are two
others—Proust and Iturri, say—who don't. They are just
not sufficiently *alive!* I am speaking to you now just as
bluntly as I would speak to myself . . . You, who are magic
itself when it comes to oral storytelling, lose most of your
effects when you come to write. You leave out the color. For
instance, your Proust—pages 3, 4, 5. If you were talking to
me, this scene would be stunning. But in your written
version what do I find? "Madame A. had a critical mind and
brought ruthless judgments to bear . . . a chorus of flat-
terers agreed . . . the conversation took a bitter turn . . .
mocking exclamations, derisive remarks," etc. Do you
realize that in all that not one word *makes me see and hear*
what you're talking about? If you were telling me this in
person, you would paint old Madame A. and her husband,
Papa Anatole France, and the whole company in fifteen lines.
You would transform your "untethered mischiefmaking"
into a single line of *dialogue*, of heard conversation, and it
would all come alive. No mere narration, for God's sake!
Concrete details and colors! And no need of summing up!
I don't give a damn whether or not you ask Proust's pardon
for having misunderstood him. Nor do I care whether or

not Sardou was "one of the kings of the contemporary stage"! Do you see? And the same goes for Iturri. A "charming and delicate dinner party"—"a conversation which wandered from one subject to another"—what are you showing me with phrases like these? But nothing! Paint me a décor, with real guests and the food they are eating! Otherwise, it's all dead! In spite of yourself, you're thinking of Madame Brisson. And I forbid you to do so! Liberate yourself! And try, oh my dear heart, do try to conceal from us the fact that you loathe writing. Try also to pardon me for throwing all this on paper so hastily. I must dash. Write me at Blvd. Suchet. I love you, I hug you, and I am determined that you shall write "marvelous" things, do you hear? My paw to Pierre.

Rozven, September 30, 1924

. . . I've had a strange letter from Robert de Flers, the editor of *Figaro*, in which he speaks of unavoidable "retrenchments," the high cost of living, etc., and asks me to limit myself to two columns per month. After making inquiries, I realized that this is a "punishment" *Figaro* is inflicting on me because I've agreed to write theater criticism for the *Quotidien*. So I replied with a note overflowing with affection, tearfully regretting that in that case I would have to cut off my contributions altogether, since the same high cost of living obliged me, as well, not to disperse my copy in too many places. I'm waiting for the reply, but meantime I'm plotting, so don't worry about me . . .

Today I've been fruit picking. It's been a fine year for pears, as well as less numerous but very beautiful apples. My head and shoulders roast in the sun, while my legs soak in the dew. The dogs are happy, and a chaffinch follows me everywhere, chattering . . .

Paris, October 15, 1924

Quotidien-ly speaking, I make my debut this evening with *Manon*, about which the advance word is already poor . . .

Otherwise? Ah! Otherwise, it's been the telephone, the Jaworski injections, fittings at the dressmaker, and the usual *schnocks* who waste one's time. And all this while you are listening to the ripe figs plopping on the ground, and licking their juice from your fingers. How rich you seem at this most beautiful season of the year! I love neither my threadbare carpets, nor Paris, nor my work . . . I only love the country-side you are living in. But next year . . .

Paul Léautaud*

Paris, October 27, 1924

I am going to be in charge of a "Colette Collection" for the publisher Ferenczi, and I would truly like to include a novel by Paul Léautaud. Is this possible? If so, tell me. If not, write me all the same to try to console me.

Marguerite Moreno

Paris, December 25, 1924

The train three and a half hours late—a crowd which made it impossible to handle luggage—a ghastly mass of papers and mail and telephone calls waiting . . . and the downstairs salon in chaos, my own room the same, the entire house impossible.

Later:

. . . This morning my daughter was commandeered by her father for lunch and a matinee at the Châtelet Theater. She has just left, hair neatly combed, in proper white stockings, black shoes, a pretty coat, and carrying three roses for her father—a very beautiful piece of work, I must say . . .

---

* Author of a nineteen-volume *Journal Littéraire* and a short novel, *Le Petit ami*, Paul Léautaud (1872–1956) was an obscure clerk in a pub-lisher's office most of his life, and then became a household word when his series of maliciously witty and no-holds-barred radio interviews about the French literary world were aired in 1950–51. Though he knew Colette only slightly, his *Journal* contains a number of penetrating, and almost tenderly respectful, references to her.

Léopold Marchand

Paris, January 21, 1925

My children, the hour is grave: *Chéri* will be revived at the Daunou Theater. Thirty days guaranteed, and if it's a success, Jeanne Renouardt can extend her engagement. Rothschild thinks we'll go on about February the 10th, but the wiser Camoin foresees that we should be ready by the 5th ... *Tout s'arrange* will give way to *Chéri*, and Rothschild will retain *L'Affaire Juliette* to fill out the evening. We'll try to get Ellen Andrée and we'll keep Basseuil. I have just sent for Guitty, Moreno is groaning to get started, and I have spent two hours making the "necessary cuts." I hope you will authorize my doing this, Léo . . . I'm pressed on all sides. One opening night follows another, implacably, and the *Quotidien* ignores their proper chronology, so the Jacques Deval review will appear before the Zimmer at the Odéon . . .

Maurice Ravel

Paris, February 1925

Cher ami, in great haste: Henri de Rothschild would take *L'Enfant et les sortilèges* for the opening of his new theater, combining it with a production of the Molière-Lulli *Princesse d'Élide*, and stage both magnificently, on March 1, 1926. How do you feel about this? I don't know if you have any plans after the Monte Carlo première. The direction, orchestra, and cast would be handsome, and entirely subject to the authors' approval, of course. But we need a prompt reply from you, and the Baron requires the exclusive rights for Paris . . .

Paris, 1925

Her Christian name is Colette, and her full name is Colette de Jouvenel. As your dedicatee,* she will become immortal! She will thank you herself . . .

---

* There seems to have been some possibility of Ravel dedicating the score of *L'Enfant et les sortilèges* to Colette's daughter. But he did not do so.

Madame Léopold Marchand

Paris, late March 1925

. . . Attendance at the Renaissance Theater has been very good in spite of the relentless weather. I don't know what it's like in the Midi, but anything would be better than the cold and furious rain we have been having here since yesterday evening. Black, icy, obstinate, stinging, it falls on a Paris so frightful I'd like to see it dissolve . . .

Hélène Picard

Cap-d'Ail, April 14, 1925

All the same, Hélène, this isn't a country for me. I'll be returning magnificently, by car, and then, finally, I'll come by and make up for not having been able to see you before I left. What an endless tumult my confounded life continues to be!

Gérard d'Houville*

Paris, April 23, 1925

But what a beautiful, beautiful review! Dear Gérard d'Houville, I have only one thought: that in your eyes I have been the woman—what am I saying?—the actress whom you described . . . It's enough to make me feel immortal.

Marguerite Moreno

Paris, May 7, 1925

So there you are, alone, and in your own domain—if I may paraphrase the song from *Noces de Jeanette*. Write me, when you've rested up. I have not seen your friends, either today or yesterday, though just now the gracious Chiwawa telephoned . . . Two days ago she and Bernard came here

---

* Gérard d'Houville (1875–1963) was the pseudonym of Marie de Heredia, a daughter of the poet José María de Heredia. She had reviewed Colette's performance as Léa, declaring that "she does not act, she lives . . . robust, dazzling, voluptuous, with nothing about her of the aging mistress at once pitiful and ridiculous . . ."

with Goudeket,* and we went to the theater, with a cold supper afterward, in Goudeket's cold but pretty apartment. I had a very long talk with this same lad last night, and when he lets himself go a little I find it altogether to his advantage. Oh, how I'd like to discuss it with you! Believe me, since you are uneasy about me: *I am fine* . . .

I'm off to my music-hall stint, my *boîte*, as I call it. And a very handy *boîte!* But, my Lord, how I do miss you! And how I'd like to go into detail . . .

Paris, May 11, 1925

Would you believe that I haven't had time to write you, my dear soul? It's the truth. I sleep late. I make my music-hall appearance. I have long talks with Goudeket, preferably at night. And our friends take me out night-clubbing . . . That's my life, and very agreeable it is, I admit. The only thing that suffers is my novel. One of these evenings I'll simply have to grab it by the scruff of its neck. Otherwise, no news but good news, and I can congratulate myself on realizing that I am still a gross creature attached to this earth, which nevertheless can scorch my flanks . . .

Paris, May 19, 1925

. . . Last night Goudeket and I had one of those talks that begin at ten minutes to midnight and go on until four twenty-five in the morning. Would you believe it? How it satisfies me to fight with a certain finesse, and to find that my partner is on the right wavelength. Does my situation please you? Orgies of mineral water, oranges, grapefruits, and cigarettes. Yes, it would make you happy and it makes me happy too. What need to say any more at this stage? . . . A burst of fine weather has just arrived in Paris . . .

---

* Maurice Goudeket (1889–1977), who was to become Colette's lover, "best friend," and, as of 1935, third husband. His *Près de Colette* (1956) and *La Douceur de vieillir* (1965) contain the best close-up portraits we have of Colette.

Paris, end of May 1925

... Let me sum up, hastily. We've had a week of melodrama. This unhappy woman,* *sensing* what was going on, has turned into a harpy and revealed her unbridled passion for Goudeket. She has pursued him and pursued me everywhere, by telephone, in other people's houses, at all hours of the day and *night.* She has questioned my housekeeper, my secretary, my Marchand friends (three phone calls the day before yesterday between nine and midnight to know my whereabouts), etc., etc. She has tried all the pettiest tricks, and yesterday Goudeket decided to speak to her. Happily, I also decided to speak to her, for a quarter of an hour before a sinister dinner for the four of us. And I succeeded in calming her down, with coolheadedness and without screams or hair-pulling. It was quite simple.

"My God, where were you at such-and-such a time?"

"Where I wanted to be."

"But your friends told me ..."

"My friends have nothing in common with inquisitors ..."

"But I want you to be happy ..."

"Rest assured, I'll take care of my happiness. And since you are a charming creature, stay that way. Don't ever believe that friendship and inquisition have anything in common."

"But you told me 'I am going to Saint-Germain,' and I passed by your house and ..."

"And you saw my car in front of the door. I had simply changed my mind."

With this tone, I had the advantage of her, naturally. She promised not to telephone me any more—to let me call her. And not to turn a dinner into a tragedy, or an evening into a sequestration. And at no time was Goudeket's name mentioned.

* Madame Bloch-Levallois, whom Colette nicknamed La Chiwawa, was a friend of Marguerite Moreno's. It was at her house in Cap d'Ail that Colette met Maurice Goudeket over the Easter holidays in 1925. There is a telling report on this encounter in *Près de Colette*.

"All right," she said. "I'll leave. But promise me that if you're happy, I'll know it?"

"The instant I am, I'll dash to the telegraph office."

But I assure you, my Marguerite, that these past six days have been terrible. I have maintained a maximum of courtesy, kindness, and . . . ignorance. Like a spoiled child, our Chiwawa only needs to be resisted and treated with strictness. It works. I telephoned her just now and she purred like a cat . . . It's for Goudeket's sake that I've shown so much patience!

That boy is exquisite. I prefer to add nothing more. But what masculine grace there is in a certain softness, and how touching it is to watch the inner warmth thaw the outer envelope. There are very few males who, without changing their tone or raising their voice, can say . . . what needs to be said.

near Avallon, Yonne, early June 1925

Acacias, acacias, and more acacias. And roses. And swift-flowing waters and even-swifter-flowing hours . . .

June 11, 1925

What am I doing? Heavens, I'm spinning. And I use this verb as a planet would. Yes, I'm spinning. I've seen roses, honeysuckle, forty degrees Centigrade of dazzling heat, moonlight, ancient wisteria enlacing the door of my old home in Saint-Sauveur. I've seen the night over Fontainebleau. And as I said, I'm spinning. Beside me there is a dark boy at the wheel. I'm on my way back to Paris, but shall I stay there? The dark boy beside me is still at the wheel, and how strange everything is! And how good I am, and how amazed I am, and what wise improvidence in my behavior! Oh yes, I'm spinning!

As you can see, you must not worry about me. From time to time I am uneasy about myself, and I give a start, prick up my ears, and cry out, "But what are you doing?" and then I refuse to think any more about it . . .

Just now, on the telephone, an enlightened Chiwawa, enlightened by the dark, dark, dark boy, sang my praises. The era of frankness is back and the cards are on the table. But, my Marguerite, how strange it all is! . . . I have the fleeting confidence of people who fall out of a clock tower and for a moment sail through the air in a comfortable fairy-world, feeling no pain anywhere . . .

Paris, June 21, 1925

Ah! la la, and la la again! And never la la enough! Your friend is very proper, believe it. She is in a fine, agreeable mess, and up to her chin, her eyes, and farther than that! Oh! the satanism of tranquil creatures—and I'm speaking of the kid Maurice. Do you want to know what he is? He's a skunk, and a this and a that, and at the same time a chic chap with a satiny hide. That's the mess I'm in . . .

Hélène Picard

Paris, end of June 1925

My Hélène, I am leading an unheard-of life! But it's so good for me. I'm coming, I *am* coming to see you! I have a hundred thousand stories to tell you, and I so much want to bring along my companion, who looks like a classical Satan. But he has to work all day in his personal hell, earning his devil's living. Hélène, Hélène, how incorrigible I am, and how happy I am to be so!

Marguerite Moreno

Paris, late Saturday evening, July 11, 1925

. . . Whom shall I thank? You, the lord of Chance, and who or what else? The Chiwawa has finally beheld us together; and all she could see was two tranquil comrades who looked like friends. Oh, the luxury of also being friends! It's hardly believable. And when she phones me asking, "What is

Maurice doing? Where is he?" I can truthfully answer, "I have no idea. We never call each other during the day." And it's true, absolutely true. We wait for evening to bring us together . . . He leaves for London tomorrow and we have just said our goodbyes without fuss. He plans to return Wednesday or Thursday—a small but certain test . . .

Hélène Picard

Guerrevieille, end of July 1925

I'm leaving, with Satan. Monday I play in Royat, and after that in fifteen other watering places, one per day. The heat and fatigue will be shattering, but I'll bring back a little gold . . . Let us retire someday to Saint-Tropez, the land of handsome fishermen. A pink house, a bit of vineyard, fruit trees, the sea at the foot of the garden, garlic and tomatoes —how would you like that? . . . Hélène, I'm becoming very southern. Just measure the change in me by this detail: since my departure I have eaten meat only once . . .

Léopold Marchand

Beauvallon-Guerrevieille, July 29, 1925

. . . The house is orange and blue, and set in the pine woods, without a foundation. All around are the wooded mountains and the sea . . . Do you know where I slept last night? Outside, on my mattress. And I shall go on doing so. Not one mosquito, not a drop of dew. Maurice indolently allowed me to try this form of bedding down and now he has a taste for it. And the sunrise on the sea, from a bed under the pergola! *Mon petit Léo*, when—at whatever time of one's life—one meets companions like yourself and Maurice, one cannot complain . . .

Comtesse Anna de Noailles

Beauvallon, early August 1925

. . . I had known nothing about this life in the Midi. Forty-three degrees Centigrade, the pine trees flowing with sap, the sea a fierce blue. I sleep on the terrace and without a single mosquito. Sunrise turns the sea white, and oh madame, the garlic and the onions in this latitude are so sweet. But I'd especially like to take you to drink white wine at the local fishermen's bar, where it would amuse you to see such handsome boys dancing together . . .

Marguerite Moreno

Beauvallon, August 5, 1925

. . . the sparrow owls are hooting under the full moon and I sleep on the terrace . . . The sea and the sand have become my native elements. So is love. Am I not an abominable creature? (I need you to assure me otherwise.) Because it's three o'clock in the afternoon, my charming companion is sleeping, but I don't need a siesta, I sleep so well at night. One always feels a little guilty writing next to someone who is asleep, even when it is only to acknowledge that he is charming and that one loves him. Tell me, wasn't it last winter that you warned me that *during a voyage* I would meet a man "who would change my life"?

Comtesse Anna de Noailles

La Mont-Dore, August 15, 1925

A city per day, four acts each evening, 200 kilometers yesterday, 300 today. I have a computer soul, but all goes well and Maurice is still intoxicated at the sight of your handwriting.

Marguerite Moreno

La Bourboule, August, 1925

Yesterday evening our receipts beat the record for twenty-five years, that is, since the casino was built! Aren't you proud of me?

Paris, September 14, 1925

. . . I'm working (*La Fin de Chéri*), so you haven't heard from me . . . Rasimi has just left, offering to pay two hundred francs per day if you will come on tour with the *Chéri*

company. We'd start January 7 . . . and do Geneva and
the Midi towns, winding up in Bordeaux. Seven days in
Marseilles, six in Nice, two at Grenoble, two at Toulon, and
that's it. This isn't a letter, it's a business proposition. Tell
anyone you know that I am virtue incarnate. My daughter
has been here for ten days and leaves for the country tomorrow, looking splendid. She does crossword puzzles with
Maurice!!!! . . . And good Lord, how "amiable" that man is,
in the most etymological sense of the word . . .

Paris, September 28, 1925
. . . If I don't write it's because I'm writing. This *Fin de
Chéri* will be my own, it torments me so. But I'm working
terribly. Maurice remains Maurice, often silent, full of
activity and nonchalance, and I love it so that he remains
with me in the evenings.

Léopold Marchand

Brussels, October 12, 1925
. . . A *very great* success. The second night, we played with
a closed box office and about twelve thousand in receipts.
Yesterday (Sunday), in spite of bad weather and the race
tracks open, we had an uncommonly good house. Reding Jr.
is enthusiastic and wants to put on *La Vagabonde*, but we
don't sign for less than a minimum of fifteen days, huh? The
company is very mediocre. Tréville is superficial but the
audience loves him because he is very young.

You see that everything is going well . . . Friday at midnight, I was dragging myself back to the hotel on foot, worn
out though having played very well, and I found Maurice
Goudeket on the sidewalk. Just imagine! He left yesterday
evening. But, Léo, what a chic fellow that boy is!

Marguerite Moreno

Paris, October 18, 1925
. . . I finished my Brussels stint with a very sweet little
chest cold. But my voice lasted through my last performance.

After that, alas . . . an abominable night, with fainting fits, and despair at not being able to get away. I left the next day, duly packed and limp, and cared for by the providential little Alba Crosbie, who had come to Brussels to visit me. It was all caused by a sudden cold wave which brought three hours of high winds, freezing squalls, and general abomination. The contrast between the overheated theater and this brutal northern winter was all I needed . . .

Paris, October 22, 1925

Now I simply must finish *La Fin de Chéri*. But, my God, how hard it is! I have 240 pages in my own manuscript. That's a great deal. But it isn't all. If you don't hear from me, be certain that I'm working well and with desolation.

Hélène Picard

Paris, November 18, 1925

. . . A word on the run. I'm doing almost nothing but working —it's my sole excuse vis-à-vis you. But lest you think too harshly of me, know that your manuscript is with Grasset and I'm watching over it, and that old man Bourget, at least, will do everything necessary to see that your beautiful book sees the light of day . . . Otherwise, I'm working—bitterly. Oh to hell with *La Fin de Chéri*. I hope he croaks . . .

Rozven, December 15, 1925

. . . I've finished my novel and I'm leaving for Marseilles this evening. I'd feel guilty at not seeing you if I had not been working like an ox. I hope the results are good—or at least I hope you'll like them.

Maurice is coming to get me the 24th . . . After that, I'll be at the Golf-Hôtel, Beauvallon, Var, until January 3. But in the interim I'll drop in on you frequently in the form of lots of pretty postcards . . .

Marseilles, December 20, 1925

. . . we opened last night with a grand success, but the previous two and a half days of rehearsal and staging crippled me . . . I'm in a mediocre hotel but the view is incomparable. When I lean out the window I get a ship's mast in my eye. How I wish you were here! You'd eat saffron rice and make eyes at handsome boys . . .

Marguerite Moreno

Nice, January 20, 1926

At Tarascon and Saint-Raphaël it was so cold that the three writing fingers of my right hand have still not regained their sensitivity. As for those overhead remains of a Gothic vaulting, with an overflowing swamp beneath, which they call the Tarascon Theater, it left us all shaking and terrified. I don't want to think about it.

Here the weather is fine, with the sun filling my hotel room and two parakeets coming and going as they please. Maurice writes me letters—but you know about love letters. The receipts are very good, the public is numerous and superb, the theater is cheerful, well-groomed, and heated. I stuff myself with garlic . . . The fruit and flower market is a pleasure for the eye, and the eye only—a dozen carnations costs forty-two francs or more, and the ordinary little narcissus, so fragrant, so divine . . . seven francs a dozen.

My little companion Alba has virtually saved my life, and looks after me like a racehorse. And if you had seen the revolt of my two parakeets just now, when it was time for them to go into their cages. The male (plump as a little finch) was enraged at what he thought I might do to his female! They were in their cages only ten minutes, but in that time they were in despair. It's very sweet. I bought them from a bird seller who, naturally, hates animals.

. . . Claire Boas* is staying at the Negresco and giving

---

* The first wife of Henry de Jouvenel, who continued to use his name.

parties. An American journalist asked to interview her for the Chicago *Tribune*, and Madame Boas consented with delight. But when the journalist saw her, she exclaimed: "Oh, but you're not Colette? I'm sorry I bothered you. Good evening."

Hélène Picard

Paris, February 20, 1926

... I'm doing *Chéri* at the Michel Theater for another eight performances beginning Monday. Today I'm rehearsing, and negotiating with *Le Figaro* for later on. I'm also getting over the siege of bronchitis which kept me in my room, and doing my *service de presse* for *La Fin de Chéri*, even though the book isn't yet bound. In addition, I've broken my pen, and I left the parakeets with a friend in the Midi, as they were ailing. In other words, I'm being my usual crazy, scattered self...

Rabat, late April 1926

... We've arrived in Rabat just in time to see the beautiful festival of Ramadan, as I believe they call the day on which everyone throws precious gifts at the sultan's feet. Earlier, we were in Fez, where we spent several days in the depths of a palace lent us by the Pasha of Marrakesh. We were the only guests, with a suite of slaves, among walls of colored faïence and "scent gardens," full of roses, mint, yellow jasmine, daturas, honeysuckle, and balm, with the night winds mixing troubling perfumes. Here in Rabat (by way of an automobile the Pasha has put at our disposal), we find the sky overcast and the sea coming in in great rollers. Between our hotel and the water there is an ancient Arab cemetery where crazily whinnying stallions were pastured this morning, and very close by, the old russet ramparts are covered with storks...

Marguerite Moreno

Paris, June 14, 1926

. . . I want to rent my town house . . . I want a lighter, more governable ship. Maurice is afraid that I'll find such a change melancholy, but how wrong he is! He cannot know how creatures like ourselves get richer each time they are able to change countries, or houses, or skins, providing they can take with them . . . the necessities, *their* necessities.

I'm told you've been working ten hours a day and I hope this isn't true. If it is, I cannot sympathize enough. Scratching paper is such a somber battle. There are no witnesses, no one else in your corner, no passion. And all the while, waiting outside, there are your blue spring, the cries of your peacocks, and the fragrance of the air. It's very sad.

My own only work has been a sketch for Lelong . . . His party was stunning. The roof garden, with a jazz band perched among the chimney pots, the lighted fountains, the banks of hortensias, with potted flares flashing their changing colors toward the sky, were all astonishing. My sketch went over very well, but as soon as courtesy enabled me to leave the grand ducal supper, I hied me off to bed in a drunken state that owed nothing to champagne . . .

Hélène Picard

Paris, July 12, 1926

I came back at eight yesterday evening from Rozven, where I gave the order to dismantle the household . . . I'm doing everything I can to straighten out my financial situation. I've spent today (after three thousand kilometers in three days, meetings with movers, etc.) with some film people, trying to sell them *Chéri.* Next I have to get my daughter ready for a visit to her father in Limousin. After that, I'll heave an "Ouf!"—though a very small one, since I must then leave for Saint-Tropez, where nothing is ready, the little house unfinished, the furniture somewhere en route, and nothing for rent in the nearby hotels . . . I seem to myself like a ship in a vortex. But what can I do? That's my life. And I can't really complain, since I have such a gentle companion . . .

Marguerite Moreno

Saint-Tropez, July 28, 1926

. . . This morning I'm on the lookout for the delivery van from Galeries Lafayette in Nice. It's bringing me a few luxuries such as a base for the stove, two small petrol lamps, two divan-beds, a broom, etc. It is with these basics that we'll move in tomorrow. Meanwhile, we are waiting for the furniture to come down from Rozven. Once it's fixed up, the house will be a delicious Provence house, with its own little plot of ground beside its own little stretch of sea, and well shaded under its old mimosas, oleanders, and terebinth trees. The former owners made it a bit ugly here and there, but you'll see! The terrace extends the first-floor bedroom, with a view of both the beautiful countryside and the pale blue sea! But just wait! . . . From now on, write me at: "La Treille Muscate," route des Cannebiers, Saint-Tropez, Var.

Hélène Picard

Saint-Tropez, August 10, 1926

. . . I can finally relax, contemplate what I've done, smile at my patio, and say *"Bonjour, mon Hélène!"* Can you believe that our arrival here was an unqualified desolation? That we hadn't a bed to lie on, or a stove to cook with, or water to wash in, not even a cool place to sit down—nothing but a local housekeeper named Louise who wept over the vermicelli soup she prepared on a tiny portable stove . . . I almost dropped everything and left. But then I calmed down and began to treat the workmen like galley slaves. And it worked—a crack of the whip and not only were the windows and their shutters in place, but the patio courtyard was done, the walls were painted pink, the electricity began to work, and the garden began to flower. In one evening, between six and ten o'clock, we planted oleanders, geraniums, pelargoniums in jars, and it looked ravishing. What fun it is to go broke! Maurice Goudeket arrived yesterday to find the house turned inside out, and nearly collapsed with surprise . . .

Marguerite Moreno

Saint-Tropez, August 14, 1926

. . . Yesterday I cleaned the roof. Lord, how sweet it is to live physically, and to feel muscles one had forgotten quickening in one's body!

Hélène Picard

Saint-Tropez, late August 1926

. . . There is nothing like this gulf coast, with its joyous land and effortless greenery. The grapes are sweet and the figs are already bursting. There hasn't been a single afternoon that was too hot, or a night that was not cool. And our leafy, airy tunnel is always fresh. It's a miracle . . . I leave September 2 for Bordeaux, where I play *Chéri* for three days, and then I go back to Paris, to oversee moving from the Boulevard Suchet house to the Palais-Royal . . .

Marguerite Moreno

Paris, September 11, 1926

. . . That was a good and lovely letter and I should reply worthily but, believe me, I have no time. My excuse: I have a piece to write which is due in five days . . .

Paris, October 6, 1926

. . . Maurice is working like a nigger—which he is. I don't see him today—or only by telephone—since it's "family night." Besides, I prefer to get over my sore throat without anyone—especially him—watching . . . My cats are charming and make good company. Neither my town house nor Rozven are rented or sold as yet. But I console myself with my little apartment, which, I promise, you'll like . . . A

six-month-old tomcat has just walked across my paper.
My daughter is settled at her school in Versailles, but I
know she is unhappy there . . . The magnificent little devil
adores the country, swimming, luxury cars, phonographs,
and dancing . . . A child of her time! And I am ill-situated
to advise or admonish her, since it is for me that she re-
serves her most sincere and discreet tenderness . . .

Hélène Picard

> Brussels, November 5, 1926

. . . I'm here, playing in *La Vagabonde*. I hope you'll like
me in it. The ten days preceding my departure from Paris
were a chaos of partial rehearsals, shouting matches with
the agent, dress fittings with Poiret,* Colette home on vacation, and a thousand other botherations. On arriving here,
we've had days of eleven-hour rehearsals, with two eggs and
a buttered bun for nourishment. Huge success, though. Today I'm resting, that is to say, I must attend a directors'
lunch . . . Ouf!

Léopold Marchand

> Saint-Tropez, December 28, 1926 (*Hôtel Sube, since
> they're installing a stove at La Treille Muscate!*)

. . . I've only communicated with you by telegram, but you
must have divined my exasperation at having to deal with an
obtuse megalomaniac like Poiret. Moreover, he has no
memory, and I have to prompt him *every evening*. He is
slow, though, to be just, he could be *very good*. If the Paris
engagement is settled, I'm going to rehearse him at his house
in Saint-Tropez. But he can't be relied on to give the same
performance onstage that he gives at rehearsals. We'll just
do the best we can . . .

---

* Paul Poiret (1870–1944), one of the most successful Paris couturiers of
the twenties, played the role of Brague in *La Vagabonde*, and though his
performance was amateur, his name was a substantial draw at the box
office.

Monte Carlo, December 29, 1926

. . . I managed to persuade Poiret to arrive in Paris on the 3rd instead of the 4th. He was planning to show up in time for the curtain—can you imagine! As it is now, he will take the same train we're taking, Sunday afternoon. We must rehearse when we arrive, and you should try to convince him that he's playing too slowly. He is ravished at being paid his thousand francs a day. But let's not mention this . . . Otherwise, all is well.

A pink-and-green mistral is blowing—magnificently—like a sheet suddenly snapping in the wind. But yesterday morning it was spring . . .

Hélène Picard

Paris, January 1927

Enclosed are passes for *La Vagabonde*. You have only to fill in the date. Don't ask me why I haven't been to see you! If you knew what I'm doing . . . I'm trying to sell both the Blvd. Suchet and the Rozven houses. But Rozven will bring a poor price. No matter.

Lucie Saglio

Paris, early January 1927

I'm waiting with somber impatience for the electric service to give me the hectowatts I need. Then I'll invite you to see my tunnel, which should amuse you. I'm delighted with it . . .

Léopold Marchand

Saint-Tropez, summer 1927

These beautiful cloudless days (not a drop of rain since March 1!) and these beautiful cold nights—we sleep on the terrace-dormitory, with the stars and the moon wheeling overhead.

My daughter has been here since yesterday—the same beautiful girl, perhaps a bit too heavy, but that will pass . . . Are you working? I'm trying. But with such pain, such humility. I advance blindly—eighteen pages!—truly. It's terrible. Why aren't we all rich?

Misz has to discover this Provençal climate in the summertime, when you stay in your wet or dry bathing suit all day long, go in the water, dry off, read, chew figs, sleep, all next to the sea. The sense of physical security is a sweet thing —nothing seems threatening under these skies. Though I'm forgetting the forest fires, deadly and magnificent to watch blazing at night. A belt of vines protects us here—vines, you know, resist fire—and we encounter the odd fatalism of the local people . . .

We: Good Lord! the forests are in flames!

Locals: Yes. It's burning fiercely, what?

We: We must hurry! Let's run!

Locals: Run where?

We: To bring help. To dig ditches, to offer our car to transport the elderly and the children, etc.

Locals (with a pout): Pooh! Stay where you are. During the fires last year a lot of Parisians tried to help, with their cars and trench picks . . . But they just got in the way . . . Stay where you are . . .

Marguerite Moreno

Paris, July 9, 1927

. . . I've just finished a moving job: rereading all of my mother's letters and extracting a few jewels. Here's one of them, very short: "Like you, I have found Madame de Lucenay very sad and changed. Since I know there is no mystery in her own life, I tell myself, 'I'll bet her grownup son has his first girlfriend' " . . . Working? Yes, but not for myself. For a collection of sea animals and plants which Méheut is illustrating . . .

Saint-Tropez, August 3, 1927

. . . I have never been rich in money, and there is no probability that I ever shall be. For me, being rich means to possess—apart from the tenderness of a loved one and my friends—a bit of ground, a car that runs, good health, and the freedom *not* to work when I don't want to, or cannot. I hear (with terror) the talk of embellishments and modern conveniences which Jouvenel is making at Castel-Novel. Electricity, hot water, baths everywhere—a house on that scale means spending half a million, and then having the delirious joy of leading, finally, the *vie de château*. Oh, Marguerite! do you hear my teeth chattering?

This morning, to celebrate the birthdays of Maurice and Julio van der Henst, we had a picnic breakfast, above a rocky beach, in one of those places you reach by a road that only leads there, and we rejoiced in the fact that for hundreds of acres of woods there were, as yet, no roads other than the paths of the customs men and the goats. It was magnificent, but it will not last forever . . .

Saint-Tropez, August 28, 1927

. . . I bought *Annales* with your charming story of the little boy lost in the meadow grass. Do you realize that a series of such rural stories written "for young people" would sell very well? "Young people" have nothing to read but inanities. And you could write "fairy stories of daily life," which would be very profitable. Think about it. Practical country poetry, with the names of plants, the hours of the day, and their colors and specific chores . . .

Here the days are passing so fast that I can hear their rushing sound in my ears . . . It's Sunday. Maurice is sleeping upstairs. Colette is sleeping here beside me. We were all up at 6:30 for a long walk along the coast road . . . And my work? Page 27, my dear . . .

Madame Léopold Marchand
Saint-Tropez, late August 1927

. . . I have a charming refrigerator, and a motorized pump, thanks to which I waste water—but then I have an inexhaustible well. As for the bulldog, she follows me into the sea with the greatest aplomb, as it were, simply continuing to walk as she swims . . .

Madame Georges Wague

Saint-Tropez, September 1, 1927

. . . I caught a little 75-centimeter shark yesterday—in my two hands. What a mug, and what teeth, and above all, what strength! No viscosity. A skin like a moist leather slipper. He was caught in the algae, unable to swim free . . . Otherwise, I never fish here. For good fishing, you need ocean tides . . .

Marguerite Moreno

Saint-Tropez, September 14, 1927

. . . Thirty-five pages, and despair. *Enfin*, I'm coming back to Paris . . . I have written Markus, who will (improbably) begin filming *Chéri* in Nice on October 15, that you were an indescribable Madame Peloux and that just maybe—if he were to approach you nimbly, and if you had nothing else to do in the theater—you might not say no. . .

Kensington Hôtel, La Croix (Var), December 23, 1927

. . . It's been raining since my arrival. It was raining even before! I still haven't seen the color of the sea, or the sun. Perhaps Maurice will bring a change. Meantime, it's pleasant to go out between downpours, dressed in only a simple jacket, and walk in the pine woods, which drip gently and smell good. It is not a bit cold, though last week there was a terrible freeze which has left the daisies and the pansies looking like pickled salad greens. Am I working? Yes, if working means tearing up what I wrote last week and beginning over.

The Saint-Tropez house enjoys the mortal temperature of all houses in the Midi which don't have central heating. But there's a stove for Pauline, and the cats and the cuisine are

heavenly—garlic, oil, and fish—so I'm content. Only my
novel torments me. I can't make out what I'm doing.

. . . The tomcat is behaving consistently. On arrival, he
struck his forehead and cried "But of course! This is where
I climb up a mulberry tree and sing at the top of my voice
and then do battle with a white cat!" And off he went.

Léopold Marchand
end of December 1927

. . . I'm in the Kensington Hôtel, La Croix, Var. Maurice
has just arrived (yesterday). After forty-eight hours of implacable weather, we are having sunshine, an explosion of
mimosas, ravishing mountains, tender meadows and creeks
—I must admit that the neighborhood of La Croix is extremely beautiful, solitary at this time of year, with pine
woods beginning at the hotel door . . .

Marguerite Moreno
Kensington Hôtel, La Croix (Var), January 3, 1928

. . . Moonlight, a wood fire, my own good lamp. What can I
complain about? Only the absence of those I love.

My daughter writes me charming loving letters. The last
contained this: "Papa isn't looking well. He has too much
blood sugar! Your prediction was right!" Sugar isn't good
for Jouvenel. He's a man who scourges himself. But I must
repeat something his own mother—the one we call Mamita
—said to my daughter in private a month or so ago. Mamita
had been ill herself. "I'm getting better," she said. "But
your father—oh yes, your father—he's much sicker than I.
I've had his blood analyzed . . ." And she stopped, with
an air of mystery and delectation. What a smoldering old
log! What a destructive flame!

For the new year, my Marguerite, I wish you—whatever
suits you best. The same torments—less sharp, less attached
to the state of health of your "bad boy" Pierre; the same
joys indissolubly mixed with the same torments—all to con-

tinue as they have been. Isn't that better than any change? I
also wish you wealth and tranquillity—and at the same time
your work. Yes, of course, I'm being contradictory. But I
am not illogical. And I love you tenderly. Oh, how happy I'd
be to have you here for a few days!

La Croix, January 5, 1928

. . . I am working with a rigor which, if it does not yield
abundant results, at least preserves a sort of self-esteem.
I have now begun my scene with the man for the *eighth* time.
It seems to me that I've turned a bend . . . But only two days
ago I was becoming enraged, and I couldn't sleep, or at least
not enough. The balance, in pages, since I arrived the 19th
of December, has been less than 40–35, I think. So you see
how it's going.

One of the hotel managers is . . . Proust's "Monsieur
Jupien." He is so true to his mental and physical type that
Maurice gapes at the sight of him. It's a pity I have so much
else to preoccupy me. I wouldn't be bored . . .

My daughter has taken one of the hardest stenographer's
examinations. Would you believe it? She's a love. And now
she's asked to go on with her baccalaureate! The little devil!
She's charming . . . The dinner bell is ringing and I look like
an old wild man. This morning I was out barefoot on the
deserted beach, roasting in the sun . . . Oh, I'd like never to
be cold again! I miss you chronically . . .

Léopold Marchand

La Croix, January 11, 1928

My dear little Léo, are you back from Vienna? I'll be in
Paris on Wednesday, returning day after tomorrow. Meantime Moreno has written me: "Paul Bernard *thinks* of playing *Chéri*. *We* are tempted." What is all this? You know very
well that I would not permit Léa to be played by anyone who
doesn't seem to impart certain stage qualities. It would be

good of you to look into this and keep me informed. If there is a Léa to be played in a foreign . . . and profitable country, it seems to me that I am here to do just that. *La Vagabonde* no, but Léa yes.

I'm coming back without having finished my novel,* which begins to appear serially in a few days. It's terrible. But I believe I've gotten through the hardest part while here.

> *9, rue de Beaujolais, Paris, January 20, 1928*

. . . Moreno seems to have decided to take *Chéri* to South America (with Paul Bernard) and is drunk to play Léa. Now I don't believe—or you either—that Moreno can give South Americans an adequate notion of Léa. Can you let me have your advice? I am above all amazed that someone simply tells me "Paul Bernard is taking *Chéri*," and not "Paul Bernard asks the authors of *Chéri* if he may take their play . . ."

Marguerite Moreno

> *Paris, February 25, 1928*

. . . No, my dear creature, I shall not be coming to Brussels, because of my daughter and, above all, because of the dinner for Max Fischer. At the moment my book is in composition —or decomposition—at the printer's, and I *must* find out where I stand financially with Flammarion's. I cannot escape this dinner. But what am I going to find out?

. . . A woman whom I helped out last year has written me: "I am suffering from hunger. Without a residence I cannot even give you an address, so I'll call for your answer tomorrow, and at the same time I'll bring you six eggs . . ." I am going to advise her to eat her eggs.

The weather is fine. I've reworked the end of my book a bit. The tiring and triple work of correcting the proofs now

---

* *La Naissance du jour*, published in late March 1928.

begins. A ridiculous footnote: I am beginning *Le Double.* Yes. Can you believe it? I'd like to form the habit of always having a novel in progress, and then too I want to oblige Ferenczi, who has been charming. My dear soul, when I talk about this kind of work, it's more or less to tame or constrain or entice you to think along these lines. I accept the idea of your abandoning the stage, but I insist that you go on writing . . . Write a novel, and some articles, and a volume of memoirs . . .

Carlos de Lazerme*

Paris, end of February 1928

Thanks to you, I have the *poncirs* [sour lemons, conserved in sugar]. They have a pretty taste all their own, not the same, it seems to me, as the insipid citron. They smell good on the mantelpiece. I thank you very much.

Carco has tumbled into your poems and there he remains. We quote you when we are together. I have looked all over the house—I'll find it yet—for a tiny moonstone to see if it is mauve on Mondays. Are you also going to be my astrologer? I was born January 28, 1873, at 10 p.m. As I enjoy good health, there are days when I hoot at myself: "Would anyone believe that I was born so long ago?"

Paris, March 5, 1928

My Lord, how pretty! Naturally, I did not understand a thing about it. You'll explain it. But it's magnificent! And what a joy to learn why blue stones, blue *glass*, blue paper, and sapphires are necessary to me. But I don't want to live with blue walls or blue furniture! A thousand thanks. I'll send you a copy of *La Naissance du jour* as soon as it appears. You'll find the word *blue* used a hundred times . . .

* The Comte Carlos de Lazerme (1873–1936), a gentleman of far-ranging culture and curiosity who published his own verse and sent Colette, among other things, her horoscope.

Marguerite Moreno

Paris, March 25, 1928

... My next book?* Page 57. I'm stagnating. When will you be in Paris? We'll end up by going to Germany, you know ... My German publisher is ready to put up the money so the affair can get started. He wants Poiret, *La Vagabonde*, *Chéri*, and a lecture by me ...

Hélène Picard

Saint-Tropez, April 14, 1928

... A true spring, Hélène, tender, fragrant, the air heavy with flowering quince (japonica), lilacs, iris, arum lilies bigger than those old horns of sugared almonds, roses, wistaria, stock ... It's so mild. And the toads sing and the frogs bark. We took a brief dip in the icy water, but the sand and the sun are already so hot that the skin tingles. If you were here you'd be dancing under the lilac clusters. On the meadows it's May already ...

The house is less habitable than last year, since eight masons are working on it. It rains liquid plaster and vocalizing tenors. You'd like their voices, and as for the local countryside, it abounds in "naughty boys" ...

Marguerite Moreno

Saint-Tropez, April 17, 1928

My dear soul, I won't be playing at the Apollo this season. My commitments are made: I am giving Pierre Brisson— if the Lord is willing—my next novel on June 15 at the latest. If I succeed, this means enormous work. So far I have eighty pages ... And since yesterday evening I have *known* that I must demolish forty if I don't want my book to turn into a dull newspaper serial. I'll settle down to this job tonight. I've also promised the book (now called *Le Double*, but that

* Provisionally called *Le Double*, this became *La Seconde*, published in March 1929.

will doubtless be changed) to Ferenczi for the end of September . . .

. . . Meantime, what weather! . . . Alas, I've just returned from taking Maurice to the railway station. He left black as the devil's . . . cheeks. Springtime in the Midi is magnificent! I had never seen it before . . .

André Billy

Saint-Tropez, April 18, 1928

Cher ami, nothing can be hidden from your clairvoyance: you have nosed out the truth, that in this novel (*La Naissance du jour*) the novel does not exist. This admitted, what a Billy article you have given me! It is such a thoroughbred piece of criticism that (despite the praise) I read it, if I may say so, with love . . .

Maurice Goudeket

Saint-Tropez, April 21, 1928

. . . I'm a water diviner, a dowser, I have the gift of finding wells! And I'm drunk with idiot's pride. Today Madame Aude took Véra and me to see her unfinished house, high up on the hill, farther than the Schroeders'. Both the location and the house are splendid . . . Sextia Aude was telling me that she had discovered two or three wells on the property, thanks to her dowser's gift. "But how is that done?" I asked. She cut an ordinary forked piece of green mimosa and showed me how the branch turned in her hands. "Try it," she said. "You can tell at once if you have the gift." But what a strange sensation! As you approach water, the forked stick becomes live, imperious, and twists like a snake in your hands. Véra tried, but she has less "witching" power than I. You can imagine that when I got home I roused Louise and Pauline, but the stick didn't move for them. So I have finally found a means of earning a living. The dowser in Haute-Vienne asks 25,000 francs to witch a well, and 500 even if there's no water . . .

Marguerite Moreno

Paris, June 14, 1928

Hear this: I have a bulldog. Sixteen months old, brindled white coat, marvelous in all points, first-prize . . . She's called Souci or Soussi and . . . but you'll see her. The breeder delivered her Saturday at five. Sunday morning at 10:30 she was walking in the Bois with Pati and me, *without my using her leash for a moment.* That says something for both of us.

Édouard Herriot*

Paris, mid-June 1928

My dear Minister and great friend, Marguerite came to see me after visiting you yesterday. She told me how affectionately you had spoken of me. She also reported your intentions with regard to the Rotonde matter.† It's become intolerable; I can't stand it any more. As I write you this evening, I am pummeled by such an odor! and crying out for help! What has obliged the Rotonde to empty its sewage three times this week instead of once? Since 9:30 this evening I have had to close all the windows, burn balsam, and suffocate. At midnight I reopened the windows to get a bit of air and I found . . . death and the plague. Ghastly flies seeking the waste matter that keeps them alive. Dear Minister, you'd only have to spend one amical—I nearly said ammonical—evening here in order to assess the situation of the residents of the north side of the Palais-Royal. No stranger would believe what we are enduring. When will the m . . . alevolent Rotonde's license expire? Shall I die,

---

* Politician and man of letters, president of the Chamber of Deputies and member of the Académie Française, Édouard Herriot (1872–1957) was a friend of Colette's from the time of *La Vagabonde.* At her death he compared her to La Fontaine and called her *"le plus grand poète français."*
† The Rotonde was a café located just under Colette's windows in the Palais-Royal. This establishment had no direct sewer drainage, and its refuse had to be collected by a special service. In the latter part of her letter, Colette makes a number of untranslatable puns on *merde.*

before then, of this m . . . alaria? M . . . isery! You're laugh-
ing at my letter because you laugh easily and heartily. But
just think of me . . . think of our beautiful Palais-Royal,
more fetid than Venice in the summertime . . .

Marguerite Moreno

Saint-Tropez, July 12, 1928

Ah! my Marguerite! What a week! I haven't written you because I didn't want to bore you—and also, my Lord, because
there wouldn't have been any place to write except my knees.
We arrived (though a last-minute telegram, advising me to
postpone coming for a fortnight, had sobered me) to find
an indescribable house, with all the furniture of the principal
room emptied into the two others, one of these being the
bathroom. No sheets on any of the beds. The stove moved
out into the garage, blocking the place for the car, and in
this same garage, Louise in tears, trying to grill a fish on a
tiny petrol stove . . . My dear, you can't believe what I
found—due to the workmen's failure to keep their promise.
The WCs which were to have been moved had simply disappeared, and their replacements were, if I may say so, not
yet *enclosed*. Nothing done—you understand? Nothing! . . .

I passed a foul night. The next morning I called in the
boss, and then, in four hellish days, I organized three weeks'
work. But if I leave now, everything is lost. You understand. I'm staying put—and our visit will have to be post-
poned to September. My poor little daughter is charming.
She is painting all the roof beams and jargonizing with the
Italian workers . . .

Saint-Tropez, July 22, 1928

It's turned warm here, but my daughter and I haven't had
time to pay attention. To make a house is nothing. What is
awful is to remake a house after a crew of workmen have
unmade it. But Colette and Colette Jr. have been meritorious.

After the first ten days, the workers themselves have admitted that they have never gotten so much done, and the so-called North Court is a marvel of simplicity and balance. Maurice arrived yesterday and couldn't believe his eyes.

We sleep on the terrace, especially my daughter, whom the sunrise doesn't disturb. It awakens me, and I retreat into my room so I'm not tempted to go out. Everything is very beautiful! The day before yesterday, we were roaming near the sea before seven and I was showing Colette the tamarisk bushes covered with hoarfrost from the dew. The water was pink and tranquil and we slipped in—Colette in her pajamas and myself in my nightgown—and our bath was so refreshing we did it again.

Saint-Tropez, August 1928

. . . My daughter left yesterday, black and burnt rose, bursting in her skin, altogether gentle and sweet with her mother, but I glimpsed all the demons of despotism, fox-trotting, fast cars, and gramophones which she is about to let loose on the three teenage boys at Germaine's . . .

Maurice has been here since last Saturday—one week. He savors the heat, the sea, and my patio court (which is charming) with a mostly silent passion—always the perfect companion, warm, full of tact, and born under the sign of Apropos.

Hélène Picard

Saint-Tropez, end of August 1928

My Hélène, don't think too harshly of me. Here it takes a kind of courage to write letters, not to mention novels! It's a country for retired people, or gardeners. It's nothing to clean my little pine woods and feel tiny rivulets of perspiration running down my back. It's nothing to keep busy about the house. But greenish-blue paper is the enemy. It gets more and more beautiful. A sentimental September is already in sight, morning and evening, over the vineyards and the sea. The grapes are sugary, the figs are bursting their skins, the peaceful nights are of a miraculous freshness— and I ask myself if my novel isn't going to turn into the lowest newspaper serial! . . . Maurice, alas, has to go back to Paris in ten days. I'll stay on—I *must* work, for one thing, and then there's a battle in progress between Alba and the rue de Beaujolais landlord, a battle that could oblige me to move if not resolved. That, I admit, would inconvenience me. My bathroom ceiling and partition have collapsed, making it impossible to live there. And there are further complications concerning the lease. But I assure you it will take more than that to ruin my good humor . . .

While writing this, I am posing for Segonzac,* who requires my vast person for his illustrations to *La Treille Muscate*. What a charming man that great painter is! My Hélène, write me. Have you heard from my daughter? She has written me *once* since July 19. She's a monster.

Marguerite Moreno

Saint-Tropez, September 10, 1928

. . . today we harvest the grapes. The weather, the light, the climate . . . If Maurice were not in my life, I swear I would not come back to Paris. I'd wait until a favorable wind brought you here; I'd visit you in Touzac. I'd make short, unhectic trips. The grapes are incomparable. But what isn't incomparable at this moment? . . . My novel is making me ill and Brisson is in tears. So I'm returning the 19th. I'll sleep and dress at the Hôtel du Beaujolais. If you visit my apartment you'll see why. Ask Alba. Litigation, lease trouble, double-dealings, what have you. I no longer have a bathroom and the dining room is a lumber yard. But the salon is intact, so I can work there . . .

* André Dunoyer de Segonzac (1884–1974), painter and engraver who illustrated a limited edition of *La Treille Muscate* (1932), a book of essays about Colette's house in Saint-Tropez.

Maurice Goudeket
Saint-Tropez, September 15, 1928

My dear, last year we made sixteen hundred liters of wine in all. This year, with a third less vineyard, we have made more than twelve hundred liters! And what wine! I tasted it this morning. It's pure sugar, that is, future alcohol. One thousand to eleven hundred liters of red, ninety liters of white . . . Much as I love you, it is only being together which consoles me for leaving this our own country. Go broke, my dear, but spend your Septembers here!

Two hundred ten pages of proofs for *Le Voyage egoïste* to correct today. And my novel? . . . With the help of the least forked twig, I continue to witch wells. I don't know how one explains this twisting of the stick, but while it's living and rebelling in my hands I feel joyfully amazed. As I come near the underground water, it wakes up, and then goes back to sleep as I withdraw. How beautiful what one does not understand can be!

Louis Barthou
Paris, early November 1928

I shall always have the pleasure of this memory: that on the morning of a ministerial crisis, Louis Barthou telephoned me to give me good news, that for a moment he left a thorny bush to offer me a little flower.*

Marguerite Moreno
Château d'Ardenne, Belgium, December 24, 1928

My Marguerite, here I am, here we are. It's a ghastly château but a good hotel. It's so quiet one can hear one's blood pounding. A little snowfall, immense forests, all very picturesque and Swiss in the best sense of the word. A good countryside, truly, and good for me since I'm working off all my fatigue. It took—just imagine—eleven hours to get here!

* Colette had just been promoted to the rank of Officer in the Légion d'Honneur.

Fog blocked the road for nearly one hundred kilometers. Maurice drove through cottonwool with great judiciousness —and at a snail's pace. The uneasiness one feels on a fog-bound road is exhausting.

Today I'm resting. Tomorrow I'll get back to work. Souci eats snow and the smell of the woods is sweet. But what silence! I'm no longer surprised that certain people urged me to avoid this place, claiming, "It's sinister!"

Comtesse Anna de Noailles

Ardenne, end of December 1928

. . . It's raining gently, and feels very good on the face and in the eyes. The entire park is starred with the white behinds of rabbits! I'm working with bureaucratic precaution and I loathe what I'm doing. I embrace you tenderly and shall return as soon as I'm finished.

Marguerite Moreno

Ardenne, December 31, 1928

Oh, Marguerite, how my work bores me! Nine hours yesterday, seven the day before—what a pretty métier writing is! But I *will* finish . . .

Hélène Picard

Ardenne, January 2, 1929

. . . I've *finished**—just a little before the stroke of midnight, December 31 . . .

Paris, February 5, 1929

How are you, my little Hélène? I'm better. But *twelve* days in bed—that's a record in my life . . . If you had seen my cupping glasses—the color of eggplant!

---

* *La Seconde*, which was serialized from January 1 to March 1 in the biweekly *Annales*. It had begun to appear before Colette had finished it. Thus her extreme anxiety, as well as, perhaps, her subsequent attack of grippe.

Carlos de Lazerme

Paris, February 9, 1929

Dear astrologer, I've just received a box of perfect chocolates. You have divined, or read in my stars, that I love only the best chocolates. I'm enjoying them all the more since I am just over an attack of grippe-bronchitis, very unpleasant at my ages (I have two or three). We've had a horrible spell of dry cold, always my enemy; I am the friend of humidity and a west wind. Do you remember the *poncirs?* I kept them until a month ago. Without rotting in the least, they had become dry, dark-colored, and almost weightless, miraculously empty, and hard as China wood.

Madame Léopold Marchand

Tangiers, Morocco, March 30, 1929

. . . The Pasha's property comprises eighty hectares of forest, flowers, vegetable gardens, orange groves, all two or three hundred meters above the sea. A beautiful house, with bathrooms everywhere. But no water or light. As soon as the master leaves, everything breaks down. But the estate itself, designed and planted years ago by an American, is twelve kilometers from Tangiers, and incomparable. Yesterday at ten in the morning we were under orange trees—imagine. They are in blossom and in fruit, the blossoms as large as anemones, and a perfume that would slay you if the wind didn't carry it off. The mimosas are like billiard balls, and the woods are full of a plant (a shrub, but I don't know the name, which enrages me) with big flat flowers, like eglantine "enlarged 20,000 times." And lizards upon lizards. And flying storks, carrying small boards, bolts, curtain rods, sticks, all to make nests for their young. If you pass under an absentminded stork who says "Ah!" or happens to yawn nervously, it's curtains!

. . . You see we're having an idiotic and charming trip, the sort which True Travelers would scorn and spit at. "To save time," we took the train. We only stopped in Madrid for a day, and finding the Prado closed, we continued on by car. Seville was so delightful we stayed for a day and a half. And went on—again by car. And saw a bit of Toledo! And then, since the cost of kilometers had devoured all our money, we came here to catch our breath. There is NOTHING to see except the sea and the Pasha's private Eden. An idiotic trip—but you understand.

Marguerite Moreno
S.S. Orsova, en route from Tangiers, April 3, 1929

My dear soul, I'm coming back, we're coming back . . . We eat all day, as on all comfortable English boats . . . Unfortunately, this one will take care of us for only two days. Gibraltar is a nameless horror. A mere glimpse of it was unbearable. Luckily, we met Henri de Rothschild, whose yacht was anchored offshore, and had dinner on board.

Georges Le Cardonnel*
Paris, April 17, 1929

Dear confrère and ami, You must excuse me. I'm emerging from an insipid assignment, long and not amusing—the scenario for a film. But while under this heavy shadow I have forgotten neither your charming article on La Seconde nor the friendship which prompted it.

Marguerite Moreno
Paris, end of April 1929

It's Saturday and two in the afternoon. Since it's Saturday, Maurice is having his little siesta on the divan. The animals —the other animals—are there as well . . . I have been tempted by an apartment on the Ile Saint-Louis, the most

* Georges Le Cardonnel had reviewed La Seconde, praising its "simplicity of means" and its "power to move and enchant us." The film scenario was for a screen adaptation of La Vagabonde, directed later in the year by Solange Bussy.

beautiful and the least expensive you can imagine: 15,000 francs rent, a nine-year lease, first floor, a salon . . . and you know what a salon on the Seine is. But how does one heat those cubes of air which dance under six-meter ceilings? I paid a visit, for my pleasure, and I tipped my hat. But . . .

Hélène Picard

Paris, early May 1929

. . . so much time has passed since we've seen each other! I'm working on overdue projects: *La Femme de province* is not making progress; a *Vogue* article has to be done over; a thin volume* of Méheut's very beautiful drawings for which I'm doing the text has to be expanded, and often it's harder to expand a text than to write it in the first place. These trifles take up my time and exacerbate me, and I find I'm late with everything, above all with you . . . Carco came to see me—he weighs one hundred and two kilos. He told me so himself. That's not bad. There was a time when being a writer did not necessarily fatten a man up . . . This week I hope to be able to furnish my house in Les Mesnuls: fifteen hundred francs of camping equipment, including three wicker chairs. I took my daughter out last Sunday, and we found four little lilac bushes covered with buds, a dozen strawberry plants, a tiny white plum tree, and a large cherry whose blossoms will be over in another eight days . . .

Paris, late June 1929

. . . I cashed the check (for a thousand francs, from the publisher Ferenczi) and enclose the money so you won't have to bother going to the bank. It's the advance on your next book. It would be sweet if you wrote Ferenczi, acknowledging receipt. I was not able to leave town without knowing you had a bit of security.

* *Regarde* . . . , by Colette and Méheut, a deluxe-edition album of colored illustrations and short texts, was published in 1930.

Pierre Moreno*

Paris, June 25, 1929

. . . Our Marguerite had a close shave. A taxi hit her car. They took her to Beaujon to sew up her scalp. She also had a shoulder and an arm badly bruised, but no fractures. The cranial probe was very painful, and there were eight or nine stitches. The dressing cannot be changed for forty-eight hours. She was, naturally, very courageous. Rosemberg is keeping her at his apartment, with a touching devotion, and has already installed a round-the-clock nurse. Erlanger is taking care of replacing her in the cast of *Le Train fantôme*. All the proper charges have been made, and the accident will be very costly to the boob of a cab driver who was responsible . . .

Marguerite Moreno

Ile de Costaérès, July 24, 1929

. . . I'm happy to have your letter. You'll be back to your old normal self when the shock has passed. I promise you . . . Yesterday morning, among other quarry, we caught two eight-liter crayfish. They were monsters which would cost twenty francs each at the market. And a beautiful lobster . . . This morning, a terrible creature from the depths, with a bristling body some thirty centimeters in diameter. He had destroyed a good piece of the net, imagine! Paws half a meter-long, as terrible as his body. We didn't know what to cook him in, so we're going to put him in an old wash-basin . . .

Saint-Tropez, August 11, 1929

A string of storms, for two days running, an unhoped-for manna, has made the countryside sparkle. It's magnificent. But how have I ever been able to work here? My patio is a madcap of flowers! Maurice works in the garden, with

* Pierre Moreno was Marguerite's nephew, with whom she lived in Touzac, Lot.

astonishment and clumsiness, and keeps asking a hundred questions. Whenever the cats see us pick up a rake they come dashing to join us. When, Marguerite, shall we all retire to the country? You have peacocks, yes, but I have zinnias as large as end tables, and eggplants that are indecent!

Saint-Tropez, September 12, 1929

My daughter has arrived . . . She will have had marvelous and ruinous vacations: a month of English countryside and London. A fortnight in Limousin, three weeks at Saint-Jean-de-Braye, and the rest here in Provence. She is exultant. Just think! She has been traveling alone all the time! A twelve-kilo portable phonograph follows her everywhere like a shadow. She has boy's shirts and the breasts of a young Negress. And she swims underwater like a little shark. And drives any car—except the Talbot, which I preserve at the top of my voice . . .

Hélène Picard

Paris, September 21, 1929

. . . I arrived yesterday, empty-handed and bent-shouldered with work I haven't done. What a winter this is going to be! And the *Revue de Paris* has asked me to replace Souday as their drama critic! But this sort of job pays very little and takes so much trouble* . . .

Marguerite Moreno

Saint-Tropez, December 26, 1929

. . . Can you hear that squall? Since this morning we've had a crazy rain, but not cold, gentle to the lips and the hair. The north room being too cold, Maurice and I have established ourselves on the upper floor, and talk about wood fires! The central heating works very well, but the ground

---

* Colette held the post for three months, from November 1929 through January 1930, and then resigned.

floor, which has never been heated, has barely begun to lose its chill. Louise (the housekeeper) keeps crying "What heat!" but it's not enough for Nordics like us. Yesterday, by special and welcome grace, we had an admirable day—a furious dawn, all copper and acid blue, and then a somber pink at sunset. And we eat under the wistaria tunnel as in summer. And we have jonquils, and narcissus, and pink stock, and frail violets, and some tiny red roses . . . And *aïoli* with the vegetables, especially the Jerusalem artichokes.

Hélène Picard

Paris, spring 1930

. . . My Hélène, I always feel guilty when I haven't seen you for a week. You must forgive me. I'm working hard at my sequel to *Sido*. Yesterday, an orgy of work from two in the afternoon until midnight, with twenty minutes out for dinner. I'm stupefied today . . .

Montfort-l'Amaury, early July 1930

. . . So your husband is dead. Peace be with him. That's one less menace in your life. If there are any "formalities," I'll give you the address of a lawyer . . . Today it's so July that hardly a leaf is moving in the air, which is at once fresh and warm. The only flowers left are the inexhaustible roses, still happy being cared for after being neglected so long. Cats and dogs swoon in the sun, and yesterday evening Maurice found a tiny lizard, surely a fairy prince, long as your little finger, onyx-red in color, with black eyes. What is this miracle?

Paris, early July 1930

Everything complicates itself so easily in my life! Now we've accepted an invitation to a cruise on Henri de Rothschild's yacht, and we're going to Norway!* It's the *Eros*, the same ship we visited in Gibraltar, and it's an enormous marvel. I agreed to go because there will be no "undesirables"—i.e.,

---

* Colette's account of this voyage, "Sur l'Eros," appears in *Prisons et paradis*.

emmerdeurs—aboard: only Léo and Misz, Pierre Benoit, Marthe Regnier . . . We sail Wednesday from Le Havre . . .

Kiel, July 13, 1930

We're only sixteen passengers, including the captain. The comfort is fairy-tale-like . . . There is everything, even telephones in each cabin, for saying good morning while lying in bed . . . The weather and the sky are silken.

Bergen, July 18, 1930

. . . The first night without night has just finished. In two or three days we'll have that midnight light which so many postcards try to show us. I don't believe Souci or La Chatte would be more uneasy and baffled than I am. At eleven in the evening we play bezique on the bridge, and nude swimmers frolic around the boat. What a beautiful voyage!

Loen I Nordfjord, July 26, 1930

You're the one who should see this country! It's an oasis for birds, of jade-colored water, of animals who are unafraid of us, of warmth. And we arrive by way of hellish corridors of serried rock, stiff waterfalls, patches of snow —the farther we go, the more beautiful and unknown the country becomes.

Marguerite Moreno

Saint-Tropez, August 15, 1930

. . . They tell me Saint-Tropez is uninhabitable this year. You only find people whose photograph appears in *Vogue* . . . Yesterday afternoon I went into the port to buy some toilet paper, and I found the waterfront barred by three rows of Hispanos and Bugattis, the "locals" in Chinese pants, and thirty people, suddenly amassed by magic, waiting for me as I came out of the news vender's. They were so cheeky that I didn't conceal what I thought of them. Happily, my

own neighborhood on the route des Cannebiers still enjoys
the privilege of privacy . . .

Saint-Tropez, August 26, 1930
. . . Maurice had to leave for Paris this morning. The poor
mutt! Both of you! Still hustling for your bread—yours at
least well toasted or buttered, whereas Maurice, strangled by
the crisis, goes back with a skewer in his behind, to pick up
crumbs . . . Telephone him if you can find a moment . . .
Alba has adopted a three-month-old boy whom she has just
christened Patrick-Henry. He's a clandestine product, the
son of a Chicago banker and a "nice" girl from the same
country—a handsome little child abandoned in the American
Hospital! Imagine!

Madame Léopold Marchand

Saint-Tropez, August 29, 1930
Yesterday evening at 7:30 the sea was a coppery pink, with
a background of white sand, and so beautiful that I plunged
myself into the water. Truly it's only here that I've ever
enjoyed such ease of living . . . The butterflies—daytime and
evening—are so lovely that I don't want to know anything
about their caterpillar stage. The great black-and-gray moths
are innumerable and as large as sparrows—you know, the
ones with eyes like red beacons in the shadows. It's terrible
to have to leave all this! This morning—very late, at seven
o'clock, too late for the sunrise light—I was in the woods and
there wasn't a sound—a silence as though the universe had
stopped. Coming back through the dew-soaked meadows, I
passed under certain fig trees . . . I don't know whom they
belong to, but what figs! One must live here to appreciate
the four colors of figs: the green with yellow pulp; the white
with red pulp; the black with red pulp; and the violet, or
rather the mauve, with pink pulp, and all with such delicate
skin. But I so wish you could know this country *other than
from a hotel*, and apart from berets, pajamas, pirate (*sic!*)
costumes, and other fakery promoted here . . .

Georges Wague

Paris, end of December 1930

But you don't need a number! Just ask for the Claridge, and then me, and you'll see . . . I'm waiting for an apartment in the Palais-Royal. The one I had was charming. But just remember that I lived there for four years in darkness. I needed a lamp day and night. Apart from the eye strain, there was a moral fatigue, especially for someone as sun-loving as I am. If I don't get the apartment in eighteen months, I'll remain here. I'm already tempted to do so anyway. Just come and see my ship bridge, my tempest winds, my perch, my watchtower, my astonishing isolation, and my view! . . . I have the bulldog and La Chatte and my own furniture, at least the pieces I prefer, and not a *single* stick belonging to the hotel . . .

Hélène Picard

Paris, late January 1931

. . . I've spent the night at the Claridge. You should see what I've done, using my own furniture, with this pigeon roost! Two rooms, two balconies, the sun, and the wind one feels on the bridge of a ship; and La Chatte, ready to have her kittens, is drunk with joy and refuses to come inside even when it's raining. But you *must* see this bridge, this tower, this mill, this mansard! It's raining again, and down below, on the street, the stream of automobiles is mirrored. It's very beautiful at night. My poor work doesn't make progress, though it must begin to do so for . . . peremptory reasons.

Maurice has become very nomadic . . . He is launched— thank God!—in a new enterprise—his pearl business is dying. Another six or eight months of tightening his belt, and I hope he will be able to breathe a little. He has spent a wretched summer and autumn. He comes back from London, leaves for Cologne, and he was in Switzerland fifteen days. My daughter, who came by to pilfer my larder this morning, tells me that Germaine Patat is looking fine. But Carco has lost twenty-two *kilos*, which is stupid. A writer must not lose his fat the way a pierced cask loses wine . . .

Paris, early February, 1931
. . . I have just come from Montfort, where I had to store our furniture in a little house next to the one which was ours, since Chanel wants La Gerbière at once, and a crew of decorators from Paris are working night and day and Sunday! Then I had to rework the scenario of *La Vagabonde* (I was paid for it eighteen months ago, but naturally that's all eaten up): The script was so flat I've had to go over it again . . .

Vienna, February 27, 1931
I left Paris in such a hurry I had no time either to see or forewarn you. I leave for Bucharest in two hours, jaded with fatigue. The program for these past two days has been unbearable. But I cannot begrudge these charming Viennese anything—they are so enthusiastic. The French minister was at the station, with photographers and reporters. There was a grand soiree concert two hours after my arrival (after twenty-four hours on the train). Yesterday a thirty-guest lunch at the embassy, my lecture at 7:30, another soiree at eleven, and today a political-journalist lunch, twenty interviews, people waiting on my landing at 9 a.m.—oh, Hélène, I'm so tired! It's going to be worse in Bucharest, where I'm threatened with a royal audience . . . and a Roumanian decoration . . . And bags to pack, and autograph books to sign —no, I was not made to put on a show sixteen hours out of twenty-four . . .

Marguerite Moreno

Bucharest, March 1, 1931
Six nights out of seven in a sleeping car! And the days! Beginning Monday, I won't sleep in a real bed until Friday evening. Great success in Vienna. But that's hardly restful. Think of me. Pity me a little . . .

Hélène Picard

Paris, March 18, 1931

Arriving from Bucharest, Vienna, and elsewhere, I was so *crazily* exhausted that I remained prostrate for four days. When I could stand up, I went to see the Marchands, both battered in every sense of the word in an automobile accident (lips, eyelids, eyebrows sewn up; leg muscles torn; Misz's face violet-colored and deformed; nothing very dangerous but a tragic look and immense loss of blood—it happened at night).... I'm now leaving for Cahors (lecture) and shall be back Monday. I leave again the 5th of April for Tunis, Oran, Constantine, Sfax, Bizerte, Algiers (more lectures). The year is so bad and Maurice and I need money...

Paris, late March 1931

... There it is, now I have bronchitis, tracheitis, cupping glasses, inhalations, and other botherations, everything one can get in the respiratory tract—except TB, of course, and it's all thanks to that damned lecture for the benefit of the Help Fund, etc., etc., that I've received these gifts from heaven.

The weather was pitilessly black and freezing. Nevertheless, two hundred people were turned away. But in addition to the drafts on the stage, as I was leaving there was a young man standing in the door, swept by the wind and the rain and holding out an autograph book and fountain pen. A Spaniard into the bargain, he asked me to write "something witty"! I was already feeling ghastly, and I replied that he could be grateful I didn't punch him—wittily—in the face.

... My daughter has returned from Castel-Novel, where she was alone, because her father and her stepmother, detained by ministerial hopes, had not gone down to join her...

Constantine, Algeria, April 14, 1931

. . . I'm a bit unwell: overwork and intoxication, of course. We left Tunis at three yesterday afternoon and did not arrive here until 8:30 this morning! And there was a telegram waiting, asking me for two further lectures, one in Mascara, the other in Sidi-bel-Abbès . . . But what I can see from my window is compensation for all my ills: this beautiful old city, covered with ancient red and gray tiles, looks as though it were swimming on an azure-blue sea, because all the vertical walls are covered with blue limewash. How you'd love the colors of this vast green ravine full of wild flowers, lilacs, roses, and—already—clematis! And the sky is as full of storks as at Rabat . . .

Algiers, April 15, 1931

. . . If only you could see the monkeys running free in Chiffa! And antelopes in the hotel garden, with their black velvet eyes and long, almost curly eyelashes! And the mother monkeys with two little breasts, just like women! And the shrimps we eat, as large as sausages! And the sun, and a flower that looks like a cockatoo!

Marguerite Moreno

Algiers, April 19, 1931

I had a very beautiful session in Algiers yesterday. What a help a full house can be! L'Opéra has perfect acoustics, and the entire hall, *every seat*, was filled. But, as they say, I didn't get a percentage!

Hélène Picard

Paris, spring 1931

. . . I need your advice. I have no title for the book which is giving me so much trouble and which isn't a novel.* It

* Originally called *Ces plaisirs* . . . , this collection of nine autobiographical essays on matters sensual is generally regarded as Colette's most important book. When it was reprinted in 1941, Colette changed its title to *Le Pur et l'impur.*

deals with old aspects of love, mixing examples of unisex-
uality—*enfin*, it does what it can . . . How do you like (for
a title) *Remous* or would you prefer *Écumes*? . . . *Remous*
fits the subject matter (or the absence of subject matter)
better. But *Écumes* is a prettier word . . .

Marguerite Moreno

Paris, June 3, 1931

. . . I have nothing to report about Paris. Storms, tiresome
work, Maurice's struggles, glimpses of Valentine Fauchier-
Magnan gotten up as a little cowboy, dinners on the balcony,
the charming face of my daughter, a prospering ramp of
geraniums, and my potted strawberries on my balconies—I
don't believe gossip gets up to my sixth floor. This open-air
life I've organized is very curious. On one of the rare warm
evenings, I slept outside, rolled up in a blanket, with my
head on a cushion . . . You must tell me what you think of
what I'm writing just now on "unisexuals." Obviously, the
chapter could be treated like this:

The Unisexuals.
"There are no unisexuals . . ."

Saint-Tropez, August 10, 1931

. . . I'm taming a pair of alcoholic hawkmoths. They sip
rosé from my palm and become drunk as popes. If only my
work were moving a little better . . . But I am dealing with
difficult subjects. And besides (as your graphological eye
may have noticed) I have a tiny splinter of bamboo in my
right index finger, which bothers me . . .

Madame Léopold Marchand

Saint-Tropez, summer 1931

. . . I'm writing you to escape from the most tiresome chore
of my life, the final pages of "the pure and the impure"—
which I cannot even glimpse in my imagination and which I
curse definitively unto the remotest reaches of posterity.

Apart from this, everything is fine, except that my old enemy, the clear, hard northeast wind, has floored me with bronchitis. But I have the pleasure of a room filled with sun from morning till night, and I can work in bed. The other pleasures of life—need I mention Maurice? no, he is too proud to figure among "pleasures"—include La Chatte and her ravishing little Jantille, the dog, the boiled chestnuts . . . Also from my bed, I'm working on my forthcoming commercial enterprise dealing with beauticians' tricks of the trade. It's very amusing and I already have some very pretty items. But the problem of finding enough capital is still strangely insoluble . . . We may end up cultivating jonquils in the South of France . . .

Francis Poulenc*

Saint-Tropez, September 1931

. . . But what pretty paper you use! You must always write me letters on large paper striped with staffs and starred with musical notes. . . . The weather here is the sort we imagine in Tahiti . . . The newspapers only talk rain and tornadoes, but since July 12 it's been blue and gold . . . We swim, sunbathe, and eat garlic, oh! the garlic, and sugar-sweet white onions, and eggplant and basil . . . Merely to name them is to praise them.

There is a typographical error in the song called *1904*. In the eighth line, it should be: *Comme Hébé qui les dieux servait* . . . Like Hébé who served the gods . . . and not: *Que les dieux servaient* . . . Like Hébé whom the gods served . . . But perhaps you have already caught it.

* Francis Poulenc (1899–1963), composer of operas, chamber music, and over one hundred of the most personable art songs in French, was a member of Les Six and an animator of Parisian musical life from the early twenties on. In her 1942 review of his ballet *Les Animaux modèles*, Colette affectionately sketched his portrait: "A big, bony boy, rural and gay, Poulenc . . . makes and drinks his own wine. Listen to his spangled instrumentation, see its golden, bubbly gleam! Look at Poulenc himself: is that the face of a water drinker?"

Marguerite Moreno

Saint-Tropez, September 1, 1931

. . . Maurice is leaving, to look after his crumbs—it would be too opulent to say crust—and I am working like an ant. I hoist something; I throw it down; and then I begin all over. The weather remains beautiful, beautiful, beautiful. The grapes are bursting with sugar, and the morning dew turns them bluish lavender.

Saint-Tropez, September 6, 1931

. . . I broke my ankle yesterday and I'm in a plaster cast! It was no one's fault, not even my own. A neighbor had dug narrow and deep little ditches beside the lane—perhaps in simple malignance? Logically, I should have broken my thigh. But what pain! I was rushed off by ambulance to the hospital and X-rays—and a plaster cast.

Madame Léopold Marchand

Saint-Tropez, September 7, 1931

. . . It's a true fracture of the fibula bone, on the slant, below the calf. And if you could see the Saint-Tropez hospital where they brought me to set the break! Happily, I was back home a few hours later—but I wasn't able to have my lunch until five o'clock, and I have no taste for five o'clock meals! I was still howling, but with hunger. Luckily there were some green beans with garlic, and marvelous local veal. It must have looked very funny to see me devouring my food in bed while Maurice looked on with stricken eyes and a clenched stomach and poor Hélène Morhange (who helped bring me home) wasn't even able to swallow a drop of brandy . . .

Marguerite Moreno

Saint-Tropez, September 10, 1931

. . . The doctor who is caring for me now tells me that I narrowly missed the most uncurable accident that can happen to a foot: a shattered ankle. When I was carried to the hospital, my foot dangling at right angle to my leg, it looked bad. I'll still be in the cast when I come back to Paris, naturally. Meantime, La Chatte is ravished and never leaves my bed . . . and the weather is radiant. I've spent the afternoon on the terrace, looking out toward the open sea, with pink lilies, vineyards, blue morning-glories, and white clouds. I can't complain . . .

Léopold Marchand

Saint-Tropez, September 19, 1931

The day after tomorrow, a whole colony of friends is escorting me to Saint-Raphaël and my sleeper to Paris . . . I'm fine. The fracture is healing as if I were still forty-five! But the ligaments of my foot, unbelievably torn, are taking longer —it will be a month or two yet . . . Meantime, I take advantage of being in bed. When it's warm, I sunbathe my foot —and the rest of me—entirely naked. Around me I have flowers and butterflies and my animals, and goldfinches eating seeds from the droopy heads of the sunflowers. The little pine woods is like new velvet. And my bitch of a cat will probably give birth in the train, or Monday in the Lyons station, or even in the car en route!

Hélène Picard

Saint-Tropez, September 1931

. . . You would have laughed yesterday. Since there were two painful places under the plaster, Dr. Frichemant boldly decided to remove the cast. But the plaster defied his surgical instruments. So Dr. F., in shirtsleeves like a ditchdigger, attacked my plaster with the help of a staghorn-handled hunting knife, my two pairs of tree-pruning shears, and a hedge clipper. After a full hour, with Pauline on one side and the doctor on the other, the plaster separated enough to reveal a soft, timid leg, which looked like the larva of a dragonfly enlarged twenty thousand times . . .

Gérard d'Houville

Paris, September 26, 1931

. . . I haven't much to complain about. This little room is full of sunlight, and on my bed I have a writing table, a cat, her five-day-old kitten, books, chocolates—and my charming daughter comes to see me every day . . .

Hélène Picard

Paris, October 1931

. . . I'm walking, about a hundred meters, with inevitable pain, but I am making progress, bit by bit. Dr. Moreau looks on and admits, now, that I had a "terrible" fall.

This book which is bitching me up will soon—inch-allah! —be finished. My life is nothing but money worries. Will it never end?

Paris, November 1931

I can't remember if I told you that I've finished my book . . . As usual, it took days and nights of despair, but it hasn't been just the book that has held up my visit. It's this bronchial cold . . . If I can make it Saturday . . . But if it rains, and doubtless it will, I can't risk slipping and re-breaking some paw or other. Because I still walk very little, and very badly.

Paris, November 1931

My silence must seem incomprehensible. I'll break it without ceremony. In the first place, I've burned my bridges: *Ces plaisirs . . .* will begin running in *Gringoire* after Kessel's *Fortune carrée*, that is, in three weeks. But there are secondary excuses: my leg is taking so long to get better. It's not a question of the fibula bone itself. That's been doing well for some time. It's the ligaments, the ones that hold together the sixteen bones of the foot. And they will take a long time, and the few steps that I've ventured here, or in the Bois, where I've gone three times, have been very painful.

Finally, in the middle of all this, I've decided, with Maurice, to launch myself in a *commerce de luxe*. One has to live. I am going to manufacture beauty products, as they say. I'll tell you all about it later. It will amuse you.

. . . This damned leg even inhibits my handwriting: since I have to hold my crutch in my right hand, and the weight of my body is fatiguing, I write awkwardly.

Paris, early December 1931

Don't be impatient . . . I've been jammed . . . I haven't had one hour to myself all week. I have had to correct, for *Gringoire* and for Ferenczi, *six* sets of proofs for my book, which will now, definitely, be called *Ces plaisirs* . . . The epigraph comes from part of a sentence in *Le Blé en herbe*: ". . . these pleasures which we so frivolously call physical . . ." I corrected the last set yesterday evening, between 10 and 2 a.m. So you see there is some excuse for my absence and my silence.

Meantime, I have a perfume that is just right, and another that will be; and a rinse, or rather a lotion, for the skin, that's marvelous; and another lotion, milky, for other skin textures. The rest of the products are late. And of course I have to have lunch and dinner with the stockholders. It's killing me, but we *must* succeed. Otherwise, life is snarling at me.

Marguerite Moreno

Paris, December 12, 1931

. . . Since you kindly offered, I would like you to steal some Max Factor products for me. The #23 for the face, and the maroon. This is for laboratory analysis, naturally. And if I could buy them from anyone, I'd be glad to. Thank you. Are you weary? Me, too . . . The past two days I've suffered martyrdom in my tendons . . .

Madame Léopold Marchand
Paris, December 22, 1931

. . . We're having trouble getting our "business" on its legs. People who have money—and there are plenty—tend to keep it hidden. We'll see. Above all, it's Maurice's torment—though he hides it as well as he can, which torments me . . . I never see Moreno, she's making a film as well as playing in *Le Sexe faible.* Simone Berriau says that she has signed to do a talking picture for "15,000 francs a week." But who knows if it's true? She's a very mysterious creature, with an open smile and a closed soul. But her beauty is stunning this season . . . We had dinner with the Carcos in their new apartment . . . Am I suffering from some sort of mental block? Or was it perhaps because the rooms are without sunlight and not yet finished? But it desolated me . . . Don't tell Germaine! But paintings on the wall have never given a room "atmosphere" . . .

Léopold Marchand
Paris, beginning of 1932

. . . I miss both of you and would miss you even more if I weren't so caught up in looking after *l'affaire Colette.* Curiosity is so great that I can't control the zeal of the reporters. They have already given me more than 50,000 francs' worth of publicity. I'm beginning to think it will work . . . In any case, the products are ravishing . . .

Your cable conveyed immense praise in a few words. What you don't know is that Carbuccia cut my text *in the middle of a sentence,* and sent me a letter informing me that he was calling a halt to *Ces plaisirs* . . . because it was not to the taste of his mass readership (sic). I'll show you the letter. Shall I sue? But the case would be heard in the civil court a year from now. Instead, I'll keep quiet and Ferenczi will give me a compensation in publicity. But no one has ever quite done this to me before!

My dears, I sense that both of you are eager to be back. Oh, the taste for France . . . That prickling about the eyes that one feels when you hear someone on the boat say: "There's the coast . . ." The truth is, there is nothing like the savor of France. I would like to spend a fortnight in that bright desert country where you're working and sighing. But I don't think I could stay any longer . . .

Maurice scratches and scrapes. We're living very modestly. The hotel has lowered the rent by a thousand francs a month, otherwise we'd have moved. No one has any money. And nevertheless we're launching a business. With a tiny packet of excellently chosen stockholders: the Pasha Glaoui, Bailby, the Princesse de Polignac, Simone Berriau, and Daniel Dreyfus. Not bad, huh? My children, do write me . . . and come back rich.

André Dunoyer de Segonzac

Paris, mid-January 1932

. . . The Princesse de Polignac* asks me to pass along an invitation to dine Sunday the 17th. The dinner and evening will be friendly, intimate, in the studio—do you know it?— with the Luc-Morhanges, Germaine Taillefer, the Carcos, Jacques Fevrier . . . Black tie or street clothes, as you wish —there will be both. A little good music without chairs in rows, and a large wood fire in the fireplace. We shall all be so happy if you come!

Marguerite Moreno

Paris, January 23, 1932

My Marguerite, you're very cruel. A handsome little horse —the sun barely risen—the weather golden . . . with three phrases you desolate me. All sorts of poignant things leave me cold. But the sound in the distance of a horse's hoofs on a deserted road, above all at night, is enough to make me

---

* The Princesse Edmond de Polignac, born Winifred Singer and heiress to the sewing-machine fortune, was one of the most enlightened music patrons of the twentieth century. Maurice Goudeket has described her Paris salon and her "cold, timid, and intimidating" personality in *Près de Colette*.

weep. It goes back to my childhood, and the black mare and the nocturnal drives from Auxerre to Saint-Sauveur, some forty kilometers . . .

We're working hard. We're at that point at which everything seems to encourage us . . . Coming to Touzac will be my reward. Kiss the twin lambs for me, on their dewy mushroom noses. And shake the dog's paw, and Pierre's as well, for both of us . . .

Edmond Jaloux

Paris, mid-March 1932

Who will not be jealous of this Jaloux?* It's perfect. It nibbles me and caresses me, and it doesn't forget to take me seriously . . . Thank you, *je vous embrasse.* But why don't you come see me, or at least La Chatte? She is ravishingly unjust toward her grownup daughter. She still licks the top of her head and her face, from habit, and then she suddenly stops, looks her bastard straight in the eye, and cries: "What am I licking you for?" And gives her a good smack. If you come, we'll lunch in the sun, on my ship's-bridge balcony. At the Claridge only the rooftops are habitable.

Hélène Picard

Paris, end of March 1932

> Either you are very happy,
> Or you are working,
> Or you have forgotten me,
> Or you are suffering . . .

---

* In his review of *Ces plaisirs* . . . , critic Edmond Jaloux (1878–1945) praised Colette's style—"the feline and sometimes aggressive grace with which she writes"—and then went on to evaluate the psychological exploration which the book ventures: "Here, I would say that her genius hesitates, afraid of insisting, and remains reserved, not entirely daring to cross the threshold of the forbidden . . ." That is, in discussing such little-frequented subjects as physical jealousy, homosexuality, and the lesbian underground, Colette was less bold, or at least more prudent, than in approaching birds, beasts, and flowers.

I stop my conjectures here. But let me know. I'm busy with my "beauty products"—the shop to be ready in six weeks, at 6, rue de Miromesnil—and to make a bit of money, I've agreed to write the French subtitles for a German film, *Mädchen in Uniform* . . . Thanks to icy nights and a window opened too wide, my eyes are purple with conjunctivitis. But I embrace you with great affection . . .

Paris, mid-April 1932

This is the sixteenth day of my siege of shingles. Its spread is enormous, covering my shoulder, chest, breast, armpit, with blisters all over the left half of my body, even down to my feet! I'm covered with ointments and scabs . . . Don't ever get shingles. My fever has gone down in the past three days. Before that it was 38.5 in the daytime and 40 at night. But I'm still unable to sleep and the nights are hard . . .

Renée Hamon*

Paris, May 1932

. . . As for translation rights to my books, it's a waste of time to talk to me. Only my publishers can give you precise answers as to what is available, since, alas, I must share any royalties with them . . . I'm opening my little shop on June 1. I'll send you an invitation . . .

Hélène Picard

Paris, end of May 1932

. . . I wanted you to see my business stationery! Our chances look good, as everyone is so curious about us. We're working like dogs!—exhausted and valiant. But nothing will be

---

* Renée Hamon (1897–1943), whom Colette nicknamed *le petit corsaire* (the little pirate), was a writer and traveler who spent nearly two years in the South Pacific, making a film about Gauguin. With Colette's encouragement, she published two books, *Aux îles de lumière* and *Amants de l'aventure*, before her death at forty-six of cancer. Her journal contains vivid glimpses of Colette *en pantoufles*.

finished. We'll make our debut in a slapdash shambles . . .
I'll send along a little package, of powder and face creams.
But my shop itself would delight you! It's entirely different
from what I had planned. Originally I had imagined something in the manner of an old spice shop in Batignolles, with
a faïence stove and a little pot to boil chestnuts, and a cat
beside the cash register . . . Alas, all that had to be sacrificed
to current fashions. But it's very gay, and very pretty as it
is . . .

Comtesse Anna de Noailles

Paris, June 1932

I have very often deprived myself of the necessities of life,
but I have never consented to give up a luxury . . .

Madame Léopold Marchand

Mâcon, July 23, 1932

We left Paris Saturday morning at 4 a.m. . . . and have been
held up by several storms en route. We're stopping over at
Avignon this evening. I can't tell you how sorry we are to
miss coming to Costaérès. But Ferenczi wants to get out my
next book (to be called *Prisons et paradis*, uncollected pieces
from 1930, 1929, 1927, and . . . 1912), so I had to stay on
and correct 256 pages of proofs in a rush, cutting and re-
pasting as I went along. Why do I always have to give prece-
dence to the tiresome things? First, the sad effects of being
virtuous, and then Hard Times. But I dream of mornings on
your island, add that smell of Brittany, like no other, which
mixes the perfume of dune grass with that of sea-wet rocks.

I'm going to open a little shop in Saint-Tropez, on the
waterfront. I won't risk anything but insufficient sales, since
a young antique dealer is taking care of all the details.
Maurice will stay only eight or ten days, but he'll come back
to get me on September 5 and we'll return to Paris by way of
a tour of our outlets here in the Midi, in Biarritz, Bordeaux,
Vichy, Châtel-Guyon, etc.

Hélène Picard

Saint-Tropez, August 1932

. . . Maurice has just left. The economic crisis is so bad in his business that he's had to shorten his vacation. He left chestnut-green, tanned, full of hidden sobs, and his pockets crammed with fresh basil.

My daughter and I have dined on a plate of fried potatoes with garlic and a salad, also with garlic. We smell stronger, but not less well than the pink lilies, and we're going to bed early. But I can't get this child up in the morning. Dawn is not for her age group. Youth is nocturnal . . .

Maurice Goudeket

Saint-Tropez, August 1932

Yesterday, about six, Jouve* arrived by car. He brought me a beautiful copy of *Paradis terrestres* on Japan paper . . . but that's nothing. In the car, he had a Congo panther, like the one I had, only more handsome, this one being larger (six or seven months old), with miraculously short ears and a pelt . . . But nothing can compare to this golden coat spotted with pure black. The face is more beautiful than mine too, nobler, more *fauve*. I locked all our animals indoors and rejoined Jouve on the road, where, on a leash and with two chambermaids doing nothing but looking after her, the panther played a game of attacking everything that passed by. She flung herself at my bare legs and we had a grand time. As soon as one pretends to take cover, she leaps with her arms spread wide and roaring with laughter. She began to chew grass, which meant she was thirsty. I opened a bottle of milk, which she gulped down with the noise of a dog, and then resumed playing. She went off to make peepee in the vineyard and tried to get into the garage rooms. She kept spitting at Moune, and Jouve, who knows how to treat animals, said "Madame Moune is nervous." With me she got

* Paul Jouve had done the illustrations for a limited edition of Colette's animal portraits called *Paradis terrestres*.

along well from the start, except for a certain antagonism. But she's terribly strong already! She's used to riding in a car and . . . sleeps with her two maids, roars if left alone, and once settled down for the night, becomes tender, soft and well behaved. She's impeccably clean. Once in the car, she played at the lowered window, nibbling at me, offering me her beautiful paws, and spitting gently. But she will attack anything that runs or rolls, unhesitatingly. If you'd been here, you'd have noticed nothing else . . . But to own and love such a beast would amount to taking orders. One would have to retire from the world . . .

Marguerite Moreno

Saint-Tropez, August 31, 1932

. . . Maurice is in Paris, where he is filling in for an entire staff on vacation or bedridden. He'll come back for me the 9th and we'll leave for Pau, Biarritz, etc., promoting our products. Then Geneva, Marseilles (international exposition of perfume, my dear!), the Grand Duchy of Luxembourg, whose entire economy is based on beauty products, and Belgium . . .

The figs have decided to ripen. Both figs and grapes are a month late this year because of the rainy spring . . . Bel-Gazou has left. We were getting along so well and life here was so good for her. But there came a telegraphic mandate from Jouvenel and off she went the next morning at five. Renaud has broken his knee again and Jouvenel has to be away, so he asked Bel-Gazou to watch over her strangely fragile brother. I assure you I swore roundly. It's taking advantage of the poor child. If Renaud has broken his knee again, why don't they hire a nurse? But you know how Bel-Gazou feels about her brother. So off she went . . .

Hélène Picard

Tours, November 22, 1932

We're leaving Tours for Caen, where I'll speak this evening. Then tomorrow I must be in Paris at 2:30 at the Printemps department store, where I demonstrate makeup and sell for three hours. What will be left of me? Because on the 25th, with a valise in my hand and a dove on my shoulder and a forget-me-not in my heart (a forget-me-not which can say *Merde!*) I'll leave for Dijon and five cities in the East . . . What a strange existence . . .

Paris, December 25, 1932

I returned three days ago, but with an inflammation of the right knee (the good one!) which hurt so badly I was barely able to move from the train to the taxi, though helped by Maurice. Overwork. Dr. Moreau says it will not be serious, so you'll see me arriving as soon as I can walk again, in three or four days. In the meantime I work in bed, in my preferred manner . . .

Paris, January 1, 1933

. . . My knee is better. It *has to be*, because I leave Friday for Amiens. Then back here and on to Brussels, back here again and south to Toulon and Cannes. In between I work on my little novel, which is stalled.

. . . Here are some New Year's Day chocolates and a "working jacket" for these cold days. You and I need these warm thingamugigs for sitting long hours in the same place. I hope it keeps you snug and helps you remember, oh my Hélène, that I am never far from you . . .

Paris, January 20, 1933

I leave at five this afternoon. Bordeaux, Pau, La Rochelle, Nantes, Rennes, Blois. I've been back in Paris for eight days but I've been besieged by a violent attack of pulmonary grippe. I'm a little better but hardly cured. Maurice wants me to stay put, but how is that possible with fixed appointments and halls rented? Just now we are passing through the two hardest months of our business—so I must go. But don't imagine I'm in danger. I'm warmly dressed, and cared for . . .

While I've been here there's been another little drama in progress. My daughter does not want to go to Rome. She claims, and reasonably, that she doesn't want to live the life of "an ambassador's daughter" who passes around cups of tea and glasses of brandy at receptions. That's no business of mine, but I had to be sure that Jouvenel would not simply go off, leaving the girl without any means of support. Now that's nearly arranged. From my bed I also prepared the French subtitles for an American film. It's a tight, tiresome, almost mathematical job. Ouf! And my little novel *La Chatte*, which I scribble at in-between moments . . . You know how my life is.

. . . You can have no idea of the weather I found in the Midi! Cannes was full of dark wind and icy rain, with the streets and seafront boulevard deserted. Happily, the auditorium was full. But don't anyone ever speak to me about the South of France in the winter!

Germaine Carco

Paris, January 22, 1933

. . . I was happy to see your handwriting. I should never have written you to defend myself against certain imputations which, I gather, reached your ear. As soon as anyone believes me *capable* of such smallness, I say nothing. My conscience is clear, I have nothing to reproach myself for, and that's enough for me.

. . . When are you coming back to Paris? I ask this without uneasiness, believing in that elasticity which is the miraculous resort of the female creature, and about which I know something. I'm writing you from my bed, where I'm winding up a bronchitis between two lecture tours . . .

Hélène Picard

Nantes, January 25, 1933

. . . We are in the hardest moments of an enterprise which we cannot abandon, since it does promise to get better. I have contracted for thirty lectures in the worst season of the year for me. What I earn sustains us and takes that burden off the business. Maurice does what he must: he travels about in the Métro and at this moment is selling bargain-cheap washing machines and a charming utensil for cleaning water pipes and toilets. So we are *all right*. I have also reduced the Claridge to the lowest possible rent, and we forge ahead.

Marguerite Moreno

Lyons, February 19, 1933

... I'll be in Grenoble this evening—then on to Valence, and back to Paris. It's not very restful—as you know—but things are going well . . . I think about you often and say good morning to you when I wake up. Then I remember that I still haven't seen your new apartment! That's very important for me. I have to change the décor when I think of you . . .

Paris, March 15, 1933

We won't be dining together Thursday after all. You recently received the catalogue inviting you to a publication party for *La Naissance du jour*—with Luc-Albert Moreau's magnificent illustrations. Naturally I am going to the vernissage, and no less naturally Luc expects the opening to be followed by a little dinner gathering organized by his gallery directors at which he and I will be present. Blinded as I was by the wish to visit your apartment, I forgot to tell you this. So choose another day for us, will you? And forgive me?

Someone has just told me that Chanel is going to marry Paul Iribe. Aren't you terrified—for Chanel? That man is a very interesting demon . . .

Hélène Picard

Paris, May 1, 1933

... I'm coming out of my nightmare, having finished my little novel yesterday. The past few weeks have been so hard that I'm ashamed. I've worked in bed, cloistered. Days (and nights) of eleven hours of work. More than once last week I saw the dawn. My God, work is unwholesome for me!

Back in the real world, I learned of the death of Anna de Noailles. That powerful presence is no more. I've thought a great deal about her since yesterday. I knew her at her best, alone, mornings, while she was still in bed. It was on one of my morning visits to her that she let her little hands fall into her lap, exclaiming, "Try to make me understand how one can live without love!"

I'm told she died of a nervous disease—of a cancer—of an intestinal malfunction. I'll find out the truth, but it isn't important . . .

Because of the corrections, and patching up still required by my text, I am not going out today. I enclose a sprig of muguet for your nightingale's beak . . .

Paris, June 1933

. . . I'm enmeshed in a stupid job, writing the dialogue for a film script* based on a novel which isn't even mine. And the hours required by this sort of work—sometimes collective— are so capricious that I don't know how to break away. I'll manage it, though, somehow—it's been so long since I've seen you . . . Meantime, can you imagine what animal crossed my balcony in three hops a few days ago? A frog, Hélène, a green tree frog! Both Pauline and the cat saw it. The cat clasped her head in her paws and cried: "But I must be dreaming!" A tree frog on the sixth floor on the avenue des Champs-Élysées. She disappeared in the rain pipe, so my story is ended. But have I ever told you that about a year ago I saw a *squirrel* walking on the narrow edge of the iron grillwork along the same balcony? The fauna of hotels is still little known . . .

---

* *Lac aux dames*, a novel by Vicki Baum, was made into a film directed by André Gide's protégé, Marc Allégret, with Simone Simon and Jean-Pierre Aumont in the leading roles, and a scenario by Colette.

Jean Vignaud*

early July 1933

. . . You have written a magic name, one which honors my own, that of Sido. It is the reward of a long life—I am sixty —to *feel* sometimes my resemblance to a mother who—and everything shows me this, deliciously, if late—was an incomparable woman. I say "sometimes," because it is not often that I deserve it.

Nor is it without design that I've told you my age. If I live long enough, I'll soon have the privilege, the right, to be familiar with all the writers younger than I, and none of them will flinch at being called *Mon petit* or even *Cher Jean Vignaud*.

I thank you and clasp your hand with a warm heart . . .

Edmond Jaloux

early July 1933

. . . One is always writing for someone. Rarely for several persons, and never for everyone. An article such as yours was made to enchant me. The cat—the living model—deserves everything you say about her. You cannot imagine—though of course you can imagine—what she does. She is so chagrined when we go out in the car without her that she has finally conquered her horror of noise, her dread of motion, and disciplined her emotions, so that now she can ride without her basket, and cross the sidewalk alone. She even *purrs in the car!*

Madame Léopold Marchand

Saint-Tropez, late July 1933

Arrived here eight days ago, exhausted, after working nine to eleven hours a day with Philippe de Rothschild and his

---

* Jean Vignaud, literary director of *Le Petit Parisien*, had reviewed *La Chatte*, in the course of which he evoked the name of Colette's mother, Sido, "who follows, accompanies, protects her daughter, and somewhere waits for her on the threshold of a fairy garden."

henchmen. The very next day Marc Allégret came down by plane to work with me four more hours! Money isn't easy to come by.

I had a visit from the little Aumont and Mlle Simone Simon, the film's *gondin*. But she's a false *gondin*, with hard eyes behind her childlike look . . .

Hélène Picard

Saint-Tropez, August 1933

. . . It's been too many days since I've written, and it's because of my work. I'm beginning to get panicky about it. It's hard making no headway. Perhaps this is the beginning of impotence. I'd give in with joy if . . . I had something else to live on. To live without writing, oh marvel!

What else can I say? Here life is solidly built around sunlight, bathing, gardening, writing, alas, and the daily promenade—though only on foot. Saint-Tropez and Saint-Maxime have become more and more Montmartre and Montparnasse. If I go into town, I'm stopped on the street by all the people whom I avoid in Paris—dressed up as Mexican planters, jugglers, cabin boys—no, no, and no. I prefer the coast road at 6 a.m., drenched in dew, and flanked by the sea on one side and fig trees on the other . . .

All the same, this peaceful life is truffled with melodramas. One of our neighbors, a model of conjugal and paternal love, faithful for ten years, at once passionate and prudish, has just abandoned his young wife and two children to run off with a "showgirl." The latter is a friend of mine, very pretty, who has never set foot in Saint-Tropez, and I can't imagine how they met.

Marguerite Moreno

Saint-Tropez, August 5, 1933

. . . Renaud de Jouvenel and Arlette Dreyfus were married four days ago, against the wishes of the parents—or at least of the mother—and have left for an unknown destination. They have been planning this move for three years, Arlette not yet being of age. They sent me a sweet telegram as they came out of the town hall. Since I don't know and won't know how long they'll have to stay hidden, I ask you not to say anything . . .

I leave you to eke out drop by drop, and with repugnance, an article destined for a deluxe brochure on digitalis, in which, of course, no one will mention digitalis! I'm developing a horror of writing. All I want to do is go on with the unbridled life I lead here: barefoot, my faded bathing suit, an old jacket, lots of garlic, and swimming at all hours of the day . . .

Hélène Picard

Saint-Tropez, August 1933

Maurice leaves tomorrow. He's had only ten days of vacation. He is now the only person managing our little beauty-product business, and he wants to bring it to a point at which it can catch its breath. It's hard. Imagine, I am going to have to take over the drama criticism for the *Journal*. The director offered me the job on the telephone. I have a feeling I'll have to go back to journalism, for a short time at least. We'll see.

. . . My daughter is in Austria with a movie company, as the second assistant on a film for which I wrote the dialogue. She worked wretchedly hard for three weeks in Paris during the worst of the heat. But now the film goes on location in the Tyrol, full of lakes and mountains, so she's ravished . . .

Maurice Goudeket

Saint-Tropez, August 1933

. . . My dinner last night was magnificent. L'Escale made me a stuffed bass and a dish of partridges with cabbage, bacon, and sausages that overwhelmed the Vanders. By way of drink, we had a very good, light Alsatian wine. (Oh, you oaf, not to have been here!) It was a lovely Saturday. Lots of people out, and a warm evening. The *Almanach de Gotha* in overalls. A much-titled fairy in a khaki cotton blouse with a workman's belt. "Fashionable" ladies in bargain-basement men's shirts. Fernande C. in an evening gown, with jewels, lacquered hair, and a butcher's mug tending to fat. She wore enormous jade beads on her arms and around her neck, and was accompanied by a décolleté gigolo in a yellow and maroon sweater, a tall, skinny marmoset with shaved eyebrows painted on again, and a head of hair like a Mary Stuart cap. Astonishing.

From a table of women dressed as boys and men with long scarves arose a tall, bony harridan dressed in cheap blue jeans and a striped-cotton sailor's shirt. Overly made-up face of a kitchen maid out of work, with a tiny beret perched on her dyed hair. This spectacle came up to me and said, "I'm delighted to see you again!" As you can guess, I didn't utter a word. "We haven't seen each other since that evening at Madame de ———" she went on, and then confronting my look of a stunted hedgehog, she told me her name . . . You'd have howled. Afterwards, the ladies danced together, cigarettes dangling from their lips . . . They danced as no one would dare dance at the rue Blomet. The Negro girls there do show a little restraint.

So I watched the passing parade. At eleven I even beheld the arrival, with male escort, of a poor, flattened-out, diminished creature wearing an ambitious panama hat and a face that was so ravaged I was frightened and pained at the same time . . . She was looking for a table. She had changed radically but I was sure it was Madame de ———. Then she saw me, said something to her husband, and they pretended to be unable to find a place and left. It was very curious. That woman was never any more than a piece of scenery, and now nothing remains. It's logical, but surprising still . . .

Hélène Picard

Paris, December 10, 1933

My Lord, where, how, in what state, in what mood are you? So much time has passed without you, my work has been so demanding and is going to get more so. Since coming back to town, I've done nothing but work, and unlike you, I don't know how to work with joy. For the past two days I've been ill (hypochlorhydria—so many *h*'s!), but I can't afford it for very long. If you still love your old friend, Hélène, send me a note—quickly.

Renée Hamon

Paris, December 1933

I adore little plants that can be kept close to me. I hope all the buds will blossom. What a quantity of work this year, good God! I embrace you with all my heart.

Hélène Picard

Paris, February 1934

. . . I hope everything has remained calm in your neighborhood.* I can't say as much for ours. Everything down on the

---

* On February 6, 1934—"Bloody Tuesday"—Paris, was assailed by a wave of violence provoked by reports of government fraud in connection with a financier named Stavisky. The rioting began on the Place de la Concorde, with sixty thousand people attacking and being attacked by mounted police, and continued for several days, primarily in the neighborhood of the Champs-Élysées, six floors below Colette's windows. In her theater column for that week she described the melee: "Like a child, one of the crowd was kicking a curbstone and shouting 'You dirty rock!' while four strapping young men were doing in a creature no more than eight or ten years old and very much alive, in fact, a young tree . . . The next morning I went out with my dog. On a bed of broken glass, nurses and children were already taking the air, and toward the Place de la Concorde young mothers were pushing their baby carriages. At the corner of the rue La Boétie, a dense crowd barred the sidewalk. I could make out waving arms and pushing shoulders . . . 'Still at it!' I thought and moved nearer. At the center of the group—pummeled, besieged, harassed, because everyone was trying to get at her—I found a little lady flower-seller, with a basket of snowdrops for sale . . ."

street has been demolished. For several nights we've been able to look down on automobiles, benches, and kiosks in flames . . . Today there's not yet been much ruckus, but it's only four o'clock.

What I want is your news. For over a month I've been contending with a neuritis (right arm, shoulder, and back) which bothers me seriously. It's becoming abhorrent to write. Injections do no good . . . Tomorrow I'm beginning diathermy.

Madame Léopold Marchand

Saint-Tropez, mid-August 1934

Léo promised me that you'd write. Do I have to shake you by the scruff of your neck? I'm working, alas. The little novel which is going to appear in *Marianne*, and which is called *Duo*, still seems destined for the stage, later on. (If Léo wants to collaborate on the adaptation, tell him to speak up!) Naturally, the novel itself isn't finished yet. After that, there's a film script for Madame Berriau, which will cloud up my summer days . . .

I go into the village very little. But I can see that this season there are a great many pretty women. (To hell with their shorts, though.) By no means the least lovely is my daughter, who is staying in a local hotel with playmates of her own age. And to think that I might have made a dozen as beautiful as she! . . . As for La Chatte, she is beating her previous records. At the order of "Scratch, Chatte!" she has learned to do "her business" on the spot. She accompanied Pauline on the train without her cat box. She walks on a leash, and the expression on her face confounds us with admiration. In the evening, the garden is full of large pink and gray sphinx butterflies which come to drink. In the maisonette above the garage, where my caretaker lives, a pair of swallows have made their nest for the second year on the shelf near the ceiling electric light. We turn on the light, and come and go about the nest, but the swallows are perfectly calm. At dawn they ask the caretaker to let them out and they nourish the little ones all day. Their second batch has just been spreading its wings . . . There are also tiny, not at all ferocious lizards, and a somewhat aggressive tortoise which I found suffering from thirst in the area of the forest fires about thirty kilometers from here. There are five hedgehogs living nearby who drink milk. And a garter snake which plays on the grille of my main gate. And toads of all sizes, who sing. I even found a fabulous seashell which looks like a black-and-white angel. Have you had enough?

Léopold Marchand

Paris, early February 1935

My very dear little Léo, what a ghastly story!* Ma-Misz told us everything, while Maurice and I made long, grim faces. If I hadn't had grippe these past six days, I'd have been the first after Misz to visit you. A mean grippe, temperature, stiffness, aches all over.

When I saw the turquoise-bathroom-1890 décor of the Théâtre Antoine, I vomited first, and then just missed slipping on the stairs. If I hadn't been wearing my flat-soled sandals, I'd have demolished myself. But I wish you hadn't been the one to be sacrificed. This is an idiotic note, but it is 10 p.m. and I have a clogged nose and a temperature of 38.2. I was supposed to move last Saturday, but I was already too ill.

Hélène Picard

Immeuble Marignan, Paris, mid-March 1935

. . . I'm inaugurating a new stationery, a new address, and a new nest . . . I do believe that this "eagle nest"—let's rather say this "stork's nest"—won't displease you. But when, *when* can you come? You'll see out over the entire city. And I so miss you.

* Léo Marchand had torn his Achilles tendon.

If I didn't work so slowly, with so much caution and cir-cumspection, I should visit you oftener. But I am so made that an hour's pleasure undoes the rest of my day. Little as I amuse myself, I don't know how to work afterwards. And this theater column takes so much time, and gives me un-believable trouble.

The Belgians have elected me to Anna de Noailles's chair in their academy. Fine! But I'm already turning green with fear at the thought of delivering my speech, scheduled for next January.

You know that when I write you a note it means that very soon after I'll be coming to visit you. Therefore, be on the lookout for your old cyclone, a little out of breath but lov-ing you as much as ever . . .

Paris, April 13, 1935

. . . We leave day after tomorrow for my brief Easter vaca-tion. If nothing happens en route, we'll spend fifteen days at La Treille Muscate. I'm terribly in need of a change. The theaters this season have been annihilating for mind and body. What mediocrities . . .

So au revoir, my little Hélène. Apropos, Maurice and I were married ten days ago. The whole ceremony took just seventeen minutes, with two witnesses making up the cortege. What's there to say? In over ten years, we hadn't found a single free morning in which to "legitimize" our situation!

Madame Léopold Marchand

Saint-Tropez, August 1935

. . . For the eleventh time in eleven years I am crying from the rooftops that summers here are the best to be found. Will you come? If you do, I'll take good care of you. We'll both get in the rumble seat of the Ford and hector Maurice while he drives . . . I'm working, alas. Maurice is translating an American play, which I then go over, but the destiny of the result is not yet assured . . . My daughter is getting married, though I don't yet know which day. Jouvenel wrote me a very charming letter thanking me for permitting the marriage to take place in Corrèze . . . How do you like me as a mother-in-law?

Hélène Picard

Paris, October 8, 1935

You have parakeets! I'm bursting with jealousy. Every so often I have a yearning for them, and I'm about to give way . . . and then I tell myself it will just be one more anchor chain. And what with traveling, and La Chatte and all . . .

But remember, a parakeet is not a bird. It's a bulldog. No nose, a thinker's forehead, and beautiful eyes. You can be sure I'll be coming to see Hélène-of-the-Parakeets!

Meantime, I'm in bed. An attack of grippe which came on so suddenly I was reminded of the days when Spanish flu struck people down in the streets.

My daughter was married last August the 11th. She's getting a divorce. Irrefutable reason: physical horror. Nothing more to be said to that! Don't talk about it. She's gone to Castel-Novel with her brothers for the burial.* I hope she doesn't come back with a cold. A cold is the almost obligatory fruit of funerals.

I had not seen Henry de Jouvenel for twelve years. And probably I would not have recognized him on the street, since he had changed radically. It seems that before a recent photograph I said: "Ah, he's done for." His wife's grief must be very great.

. . . Back to the parakeets: Don't let them get cold! They catch pneumonia so easily. I still remember my mother's parakeets, which were green. If the cage is too small, I'll give you another. And do they have a nesting place?

---

* Henry de Jouvenel had died the night of October 5–6, after suffering a stroke as he walked home from the Automobile Show.

Paris, January 3, 1936

. . . Parakeets throughout their lives need to trim their beaks, that is to say, prevent them from growing too large. If this happens, their mandibles—the upper and lower bills —get in each other's way and the parakeet is unable to eat. I shudder at the very thought of such a thing happening. They gnaw at their cage when they have nothing else. Give them sticks or hazelnuts. I'll send you some very hard Brazil nuts. You'll see what happens . . . Do they like fruit? I wouldn't be surprised. They need green as well as dry food, just as we do. I'm eager to see all three of you, but there are so many impediments keeping me away! Maurice and I have had to translate an American play.* It is not certain that it will be produced, but you understand, it must be ready . . . You've no idea what a crisis there is in book sales . . .

Renée Hamon

Paris, January 13, 1936

Thank you, my little Renée. The daphnes have arrived, fresh and intact, and their fruity odor fills the room where I am writing. Eight days ago, I was given another rarity, some branches of a Japanese plant with large purple flowers, called chimonanthus, so I have two miraculously scented plants which blossom from December through January. Thank you again and happy New Year. I hope you are prospering and that you will come by and disturb my work, which wearies me.

Léopold Marchand

Paris, January 23, 1936

My little Léo, thank you. Thank God the four of us love each other. You won't be angry to learn that the telegraphist emasculated you. In your message, you were *si heureuse* and signed yourself *Votre petite Léo*. The telegraph service can-

---

* *The Royal Family*, by George S. Kaufman and Moss Hart.

not imagine a Commandeur* receiving tender greetings from anyone but a woman! . . .

Hélène Picard

Paris, April 1, 1936

I'm about to leave for Brussels. The Royal Academy will receive me Saturday and need I tell you that I'm nothing but misanthropy, anguish, stomachache, stammering, and general collapse? I come back the 8th, and won't be happy until I've called to tell you my adventures as a "recipient."

This entire month has been desolating. I'll send you my acceptance speech, which I groaned over: it certainly isn't the work I was born for . . .

Madame Léopold Marchand

Saint-Tropez, April 1936

It's pouring wistaria blossoms . . . and drops of rain. I only want to assure you both that we are thinking of you, that we've arrived, and that La Chatte was fantastic throughout the trip, roaring with laughter and eating at the table with us at every stop . . . The garden is full of moist flowers, but the little wood is flooded . . .

Renée Hamon

Saint-Tropez, August 1, 1936

It's a tough break, my poor little pirate! But there you are, picking up the pieces already, because you're a good sort. Stick them back together, my child—it's a woman's job.

As for my daughter, don't count on her. She's decisive only when she's talking. She's a charming child, and I adore her, but she tends to "abuse" time rather than make "use" of it. I should have seen to it that she was born rich! Her eagerness to travel will settle for a month in the South of France, I daresay. Of course there are other factors—she

---

* On January 21, Colette had been promoted to the rank of Commandeur in the Légion d'Honneur.

has no money and she's hoping to get an assistant director's job on the Saint-Exupéry film . . .

I'm working terribly hard, every day, every day, in spite of the beautiful weather. I have to bring back over a hundred pages of a finished novella for the September *Gringoire*. I hope I won't be too far behind. Meantime, I'm waiting with relish for the Brittany cakes . . . to lose weight.

This isn't the moment to forget to wish "Good luck to the little pirate!" and to hug her with all my heart. Bravo for the article . . . You'll have your islands yet—oh yes! . . .

Hélène Picard

Saint-Tropez, September 15, 1936

I'm coming back, my Hélène. We'll be in Paris by Monday. This week *Gringoire* will begin *Bella-Vista*, the lean fruit of my vacation, which will probably run for four issues . . .

These humid September evenings have brought out the toads, which are enormous down here. But we also have tiny pine toads, the size of bumblebees, marvels of tooling and almost all black. We saved the life of one of the large toads, which had fallen into a ditch and was clutching on to twigs, like a human being. A large green lizard dropped out of a tree and onto my neck. And a green-and-maroon snake kidnapped a neighbor's chicken. "I shouted and shouted at it," said my neighbor, "but it wouldn't let go. Not even when I threw a stick at it!" Finally it did let go but by then the chick was dead. Our jungle is peopled, as you can see . . .

Marguerite Moreno

Paris, October 6, 1936

It's stupid of me, Marguerite. I wanted to send you the *Journal* article in which I had the pleasure of naming you before reviewing the show at the Madeleine. But my copy has disappeared and I can't find it. I'm writing you all the same. You are magnificent in your scene. What a lesson, what a number of lessons, you give actors and actresses in our time! Maurice was ravished.

Hélène Picard

Paris, early January 1937

Our letters must have crossed again. Our hearts as well. Don't think badly of me if I leave for Nice without coming to call on you. I've had another attack of grippe and I need a change of air. I won't go to Saint-Tropez, it will be too cold there. I'll settle for a banal hotel in Nice, an open window, and eight days of loafing. Maurice won't have the time to come along, he is directing and editing a new weekly called *Confessions* with the Kessel brothers. It's in its fifth week and looks as though it might survive . . .

Marguerite Moreno

Paris, July 13, 1937

Magnificent! Yesterday evening I saw your film of *La Dame de pique*. You are a striking lesson in what an actor should do. When I see actors playing old age, especially on the stage, I want to vomit. Your performance was exemplary— your feebleness at the end, the grace of your mischiefmaking. And then for once it's a real part, a role that begins somewhere and goes somewhere. Why hasn't a play ever been made of it? Or is there one? Even so, it won't exist until you've played in it . . .

Hélène Picard

Paris, December 6, 1937

On the 10th of this month, at the *Annales*, I'm giving myself the joy of talking about you, and Suzanne Després will read your parakeet poem. It won't be worthy of you, but that would require an entire lecture devoted to you, and not just five minutes' fervor. Meantime, I hug you. I'm working, but what will become of writers? Books are selling so badly. I'm sending you a new collection of short stories, *Bella-Vista*. And my tenderness for you remains unchanging . . .

Paris, December 11, 1937

Great success for you and the parakeets! Tomorrow I'll repeat the performances for foreign students. I don't get paid, but they're so sweet. As soon as my text is copied, I'll send it to you . . .

Renée Hamon

Paris, December 24, 1937

. . . This morning I received the good, salty little griddle cakes, as 100 percent Breton as you yourself, and everything leads me to believe that they won't last very long . . .

Here it's dark gray. The transport workers are on strike. Books are selling badly. We certainly need a desert isle. And there you are, watching an aged creature slowly, bit by bit, detach itself from life. It's sad. We don't really know why it's sad, but it gives us pain. When she is gone, you'll no longer have any deep or concrete bond with your part of the world. Where to find an anchor then? In your work. I understand that well enough, but I also understand that there are hours when one no longer even has an anchor to drop overboard. But don't think about that today. Are you having good weather? Brittany is often so warm at this time of year. In February I have not only seen violets but hawthorn in great white clouds, and blue hyacinths in the grass of the little coves . . .

Edmond Jaloux

Paris, end of December 1937

And I who hold myself back, tie myself in knots, bridle, muzzle, strangle, and gag myself—all to avoid those "tragic" effects which come too easily!* The next time . . . But you have given me a charming Jaloux. I emerge from my winter

---

* Reviewing *Bella-Vista*, Edmond Jaloux had praised Colette's art of "depicting troubled characters," but at the same time found the title story disappointing. He added, however, that her style remained "incomparable."

hibernation to tender you a paw which the cold has stiffened but your friendship warmed again. The weather horrifies me. In a fortnight, will you come see us in the Palais-Royal? Happy New Year from both of us to both of you. I nuzzle you with a cold nose.

Charles and Lucie Saglio

Palais-Royal, Paris, January 1938

We're exhausted, but we're finally in the Palais-Royal! What a consolation, and into the bargain, in the center of a round table, there is your round basket of red tulips, to comfort both soul and eye. Thank you, bless you, both.

Come and see my view! Right now, any time! These apartments on the quadrangle are never very comfortable. But what a sealed-off world! Madame Massé sends me baked pears, the bistro across the street delivers a pair of stuffed crêpes, the antique dealer climbs the stairs with greetings and sticks of incense, and the garden caretaker, seeing me with the dog unleashed, cries: "But you're incorrigible!" The lampshade maker wipes a tear. The excellent restaurateur at the Roi Louis XIV tells me: "You've come to find us again? We use to be located in the rue du Cherche-Midi . . ." Find me a neighborhood like this! And the coal dealer in the rue Chabanais, who is another old acquaintance!

Dear Charles and Lucie, we must dine together at the bistro in question. On Tuesdays there is a *cassoulet* and the wines are regional. How about Tuesday?

Renée Hamon

Paris, February 25, 1938

My little Renée, the odor of the laurel blossoms is extraordinary. It behaves like almost all intense perfumes, it rests at certain hours. But it is diurnal, whereas the tuberoses and the lilies are nocturnal, and become maddened between midnight and four in the morning.

Work, *mon vieux*, work. I'm tugging away at a story for *Marie-Claire*. And I find it very hard. What I really need is some clean, salt air. Though I can't complain about the sunlight coming in the window this minute as though it were at home here. The state of the weather has always had a large place in my life. Imagine, the first thing I look for in the newspaper is the weather forecast.

Nothing earthshaking to report. Men are talking about war. But an old woman like myself, to whom yet another war would only mean sitting tight and at best dying without fuss, takes less interest in such matters. Are you all right? Is the gentle Brittany climate consoling you as you wait for your grandmother's death? I embrace you, little pirate, and thank you for the laurel. It's midnight: time to put on your little pink knitted bed jacket!

Henri Mondor*

Paris, April 14, 1938

Yesterday evening I finished a long story called *Le Toutounier*. And I have not forgotten that you asked me for a list of my available manuscripts. I have the following ones here, on various blue paper:

La Chatte
Ces plaisirs . . .
Bella-Vista
La Seconde
Sido
Duo

as well as the *Claudines*. Perhaps I am forgetting some, but I would especially like to show you the *Claudines*. Let's make a date, when you have a few free hours . . .

---

* Dr. Henri Mondor (1885–1962) combined a brilliant career as a surgeon—in June 1938 he removed Colette's daughter's appendix—with that of man of letters and Mallarmé specialist.

Paris, June 6, 1938

. . . Since our lunch, I have done nothing but think about the quasi-symbolic rivalry between Dance and Love.* To speak frankly, my instinct has always been to flee the symbol, which leaves me cold. And I lose all my ease when I try to work from someone else's synopsis. It isn't from any lack of goodwill, especially in this case, when I would have the satisfaction of demonstrating my friendship for you. I simply dry up. A writer can have limitations, impotences, but also, thank God, a clear conscience. I count on you to help Mlle Chauviré to understand this.

On the other hand, once the script was developed by someone more expert than myself, nothing would prevent my writing the dialogue. That, however immodest it may be for me to say so, is my proper métier. I am thus capable of preferring my scruples to any profit—which gives me a melancholy sort of pleasure. I am not proud—it is just my way of feeling myself intact . . .

Madame Léopold Marchand

Saint-Tropez, July 15, 1938

Since I don't know just where you are, I'm writing to Paris. Besides, I have nothing much to tell you, volumes of nothing. The weather is the sort I cannot describe. Heat and freshness at the same time. To dine in the shade at noon, you need a shawl. The sea isn't warm enough to stay in very long. The garden is a tempest compacted of flowers and shrubbery. To leave the scorched fields up north and arrive here to find fields still full of spring grass and flowers is fantastic . . .

The day we arrived, the Windsors had come from Antibes by boat, to return two alabaster vases to an antique dealer

---

* On behalf of an actress named Yvette Chauviré, Dr. Mondor had proposed to Colette that she write a film script based on the life of the nineteenth-century dancer who had inspired the ballet *Giselle*. But Mlle Chauviré wanted a more romantic treatment than Colette found compatible with her taste.

friend. But maritime law requires that any article of trade taken off a ship have a stamped and signed authorization. The local customs inspector was zealous for his part. "Good," said Windsor. "Where is the man who signs the paper?" He was sent for, but he was eating lunch and refused to leave the table. "Eh, I have to eat, don't I? Can't they wait for me, like anyone else?" The delirious population surrounded the dock where the boat was moored, and time passed. Windsor, who used to have so much fun in Saint-Tropez, was furious and swore he'd never set foot in the place again. But the law was respected. What surprised me was that it apparently never occurred to Windsor simply to keep the vases, which were worth only a hundred francs each . . .

Renée Hamon

Paris, September 25, 1938

That's all very good, little pirate, and I add my congratulations to the Colonial Minister's!*

. . . I don't want to go back to the South of France for the summer. I have a terrible longing for Brittany. Send me information on the hotel where you are staying. Summer prices, restaurant service, nature of the guest list. Is it near the water? A decent beach? Rocks, sand? No radios? If there is a publicity folder with photographs, send this, please.

Paris, October 17, 1938

It's hard to give you a precise answer. *Paris-Soir* wants to use me for every possible sort of assignment. Not only am I going to have to go to Fez in November to cover the Oum-El-Hassen trial, but in June I'll have to do a month-long series on summer in France. So, you see, I dare not reserve a villa now which I may not be able to use until next July . . . I have no idea what to do!

---

* On returning from the Marquesas Islands, Renée Hamon had submitted a report on local sanitary conditions to the Colonial Minister, which had resulted in the government instituting state medical service.

Géraldy's play has gotten off to a good start.* The actors are good. I only hope it doesn't fall on its face too soon. I'm writing this hastily. This evening I must trim a story that's already too short, for America . . .

Léopold Marchand

Fez, November 10, 1938

Hello, my little Léo. I'm writing you because it's raining and that's when one most misses the people one loves. The garden of this Palais-Jamaï is magnificent, with datura flowers fifty centimeters long and funnel-shaped blossoms that open like old-fashioned phonograph horns. The trial doesn't begin until Monday and in the meantime we're trying to get a little background. We've been coming here for thirteen years and the little sparrow hawks are still perched on the highest branches of the poplars. But the Fez water supply has been purified, making for a funny situation, since formerly when a traveler ordered "My chocolate!" they ran him a bath. Ha-ha-ha . . .

Hélène Picard

Paris, December 4, 1938

. . . I'm working with perfect humility. In the past fortnight, apart from my weekly *Paris-Soir*, I have to my credit a publicity text for a tobacco firm, the introduction to a new edition (enchanting) of flowers painted by Redouté, the proofs for *Le Toutounier* (which you'll have as soon as it's out), and other scraps to keep my stove warm. As for Maurice . . . But you know this old refrain, and how virtuously we carry on.

Renée Hamon

Paris, December 14, 1938

. . . Finally I can see clearly enough ahead to make plans. Another two weeks' work and then! Maurice and I shall

---

* Paul Géraldy's stage adaptation of Colette's 1934 novel *Duo* had opened on October 10.

come by car in spite of the shortening days, on the 24th or perhaps the 23rd. Moune Morhange and Luc-Albert Moreau will come by train. And now Géraldy and his friend Antoinette Sachs want to come as well. These six persons would like to stay four days, six days (us), three days. Maurice and I would want two rooms, or a small apartment with bath. I'm not sure about the others, but I doubt if they sleep two in the same room. I'll let you know.

All I ask of Madame Pollez is that she distinguish herself with plenty of heat. And find me an electric desk lamp, since I'll have to scribble while I'm there. Also: are the nuns who teach deaf-mutes to speak and hear still in the neighborhood? (This for a *Paris-Soir* article.) And let there be a free day on which I can see Belle-Isle again!

That's the present state of our great project. Maybe we'll even get to a midnight mass?

Paris, December 21, 1938

Oh yes, it's a disaster. Everything's bursting. The roads are snow and mud, mixed. I confine myself to the fireplace, the divan, and the lamp. Nothing to do about it. Just tell me when the hotel reopens in January. When the weather improves, it will be even nicer in Brittany, and we'll celebrate New Year's on whatever day I arrive. But tell Madame Angèle that, even on moderately cold days, I shall gladly pay for supplementary heat.

The Palais-Royal hasn't looked this way since Richelieu. Heavy snow everywhere, frozen solid, with no sign of thaw.

Work hard and wait for us. A cloud of snow has begun to swirl outside again. It's very beautiful to look at, but . . .

Paris, December 24, 1938

Little pirate, it's not a question of the railway or the car or anything of the sort. It's a question of cold, which is cruel to me. To come to Auray simply to watch the cold outside the window is neither possible nor desirable. I want that warm Brittany air, which one so often finds in the winter, and the freedom to walk. And I'll have it. Let's wait.

Yesterday the chocolates arrived, and an excellent pâté! This is your doing, little pirate—you're incorrigible. I'm revenging myself by sending you a belt—a very pirate-like belt—from Hermès. Let me know if it gets there promptly.

À bientôt, my child. Merry Christmas, Merry Christmas! We are your old friends who hug you tight.

Paris, January 19, 1939

Attention! Things are shaping up!

I'm getting over a sort of grippe and I'm not worth a cent. If we arrive the 26th (impossible before), will that be convenient?

Old Souci, the waning Chatte, Maurice, and I are dearly in need of a change of air. And if Madame Pollez asks an additional charge for heat, we'll willingly comply . . .

If there isn't a work lamp, buy me a practical one, will you? I'll also need some sand for the cat box.

Paris, January 26, 1939

The trip's put off again! Apart from the ghastly weather, there are deadlines. The last one falls on the 31st. On that day—and even before—I'll send you an irrevocable telegram, and we'll arrive the 3rd . . .

Paris, January 30, 1939

Never mind—I'll come by train! Otherwise, I'll never get there. Maurice speaks on the radio on the 6th, so I'll leave him to come when he can. If we want to go out, we'll use a taxi. I'll carry the cat box, and you will buy me a good slice of veal liver (raw). My poor dear cat is slowly emerging from a crisis of aging which I thought she would not survive. She was cured with the help of raw veal liver and now she's getting better. But she weighs nothing. The sea air will do her good. I too am all shoddy, heavy, and aged 101 . . .

You know better than I the arrival time of the afternoon

train. Can someone be there to take my suitcase, blankets, beasts, and all? You understand I must come now. On the 14th I have a dinner of the Belgian Literary Academy at which I must preside. So I'm getting out . . . In any case, you'll have a telegram announcing that I'm en route!

Paris, February 1, 1939

[*Telegram*] Everything is changed and rearranged. We'll arrive the evening of the 7th. Affectionately

Madame Léopold Marchand

La Trinité-sur-Mer, early February 1939

My dear children, what beautiful weather! And I'm rediscovering this Brittany quality of air, and its precocious spring, and forgotten seashells. Marvelous food—huge shrimps, clams, oysters, salt butter, everything. I had such a desperate need of this little cure, it's making me tipsy. Tenderness.

Renée Hamon

Paris, February 22, 1939

My little pirate, it's all over for La Chatte. The veterinary said I should have intervened sooner because it was cancer.

We won't mention it again.

In my *Paris-Soir* piece on the deaf-mutes, the printer put in *yeux purs* [pure eyes] instead of "*yeux pers*" [sea-green eyes]. People have committed suicide for less . . .

Paris, March 19, 1939

What a dirty business being a "crime reporter" is. Though it's true that Weidmann's confession* was worth losing the

---

* Eugene Weidmann was the last man to be publicly beheaded in France. Colette's account of his murder trial is included in *Belles Saisons*. In *Paris Was Yesterday*, Janet Flanner reports that Colette's "brilliant appreciative essay on the murderer's spiritual capacity for truth honored Weidmann with fine writing such as she has hitherto bestowed only on nature and animals."

time to hear. But please notice, my little pirate, that between court sessions I had three days of false grippe, or hyper-chlorhydria (what a word!), which will help to explain my silence. Don't worry about the preface for your book. It will be done on time.

Would you believe that I have a rendezvous with a property owner in La Trinité? He would rent for three months. His grounds are near the large beach where we went to gather shells, do you remember? He and his photographs are coming Tuesday . . .

Paris, March 20, 1939

My little Renée, the dog died last night. A hideous epilepsy. An earlier crisis warned me eight days ago. What is strange is that La Chatte died on a Sunday, the 19th of February, and the dog on a Sunday, the 19th of March.

I attach the little letter-preface for your book, which I have just finished. As you'll see, I'm pretending that I am writing to you, before your return voyage, before you've written your book. This enables me to assume an affectionate and even counseling tone. I hope it will satisfy you and your publisher and that it will make me a little bit responsible for your book . . .

Madame Léopold Marchand

Château d'Alizay, May 1939

Ma-Misz, this is not really a château. It's a small Restoration house whose proprietor I've known for years. His name is Marcel, he's only fifty-seven, and he and his mother used to be close friends of my mother-in-law, the blessed Marie de Jouvenel. Marcel's "associate"—if I may put it so—does the cooking, very good, simple cooking, and it's close to Paris. Perhaps Léo might use Alizay for a period of intensive work.

As for work, we're up to our ears. Especially Maurice, who is writing a series of articles for *Paris-Soir*. Our life is perfectly austere. But we go out for a drive in the morning, through a countryside which is all flowers and fresh—even chilly—air. Rouen is eighteen kilometers away. So, you see, I'm behaving myself, but I would like to glimpse the end of this novella I'm struggling over. I don't ask you to write to me, my dears, but the least profile of our Léo as a bishop, or a catfish, or Belle Otéro, or a country constable, would give me great pleasure. And the Big Little Cat? There's a striped one here, and two little ones, and a slightly spoiled dog imitating a panda.

The estates in this region are fantastic, deserted mostly, and evoking an era when people believed they were rich, surrounding their hundreds of acres with walls that loftily separated them from roads or their neighbors. They're astonishing to see. Alfred Bloch's is not far away.

What a letter! It's a quarter to seven in the morning and I've already lighted my wood fire. I'm looking out over dew-drenched meadows and waiting for the breakfast bell. Maurice worked late last night and is still asleep in his room. Ma-Misz and Léo, I hug you both.

Renée Hamon

Alizay, May 15, 1939

Ma petite Renée, my daughter lives at 5, rue de Lille, phone Littré 79-80. This is the briefest note, as we are going into Rouen to buy ink, a hot-water bottle, and other essentials. I'll be very happy when you're back in your own vital element, the high seas. But I doubt if you'll stir Bel-Gazou from her fixed habits. Try anyway. It's indescribably cold here . . .

Georges Mandel

Paris, June 1, 1939

Monsieur le Ministre, cher ami, I know that your magical memory has not forgotten Renée Hamon. For the second time in a year I am putting her in your hands. Since you will not have forgotten her, you know that the destiny of this energetic little galvanizer is not here but "down under." Counting on the special friendship you have always shown me, I would like to finish this letter by saying, "Give Renée Hamon what she needs." But I think it more discreet—and perhaps more advantageous—simply to say, "Give Renée Hamon what you deem good."

Jean Fraysse

Paris, early June 1939

Dear Jean, it's still me. The young woman who brings you this letter is Renée Hamon. To explain just who Renée Hamon is would take a long time—I'll leave that to her. She'll know how to be brief. She is just back from the antipodes and travel is her life. She has a film, two films, she has precise remembrances, picturesque and without fancy trimmings. What she doesn't have is a means of livelihood. Mandel has been kind to her—and will continue to be. But for the moment, for her daily bread, rented room, and the rest, could you possibly find her a little place on the radio? Colonial propaganda is not unuseful at this time. Renée Hamon has made broadcasts and can do so again . . . I leave her in your good hands, knowing from experience how effective they can be . . .

Renée Hamon

Paris, June 9, 1939

You're a gutsy girl. You handled yourself very well yesterday and I was proud of you as I read the Fouqueray review in the *Journal* this morning. I'm leaving for Saint-Tropez with Maurice tonight, but we'll be returning Tuesday. Then I'll give you a few pointers on your talk. The delivery was a bit slow at the beginning. Give it a little more of a conversational tone. I'll show you a trick or two when I'm back. It'll come easily. With the right intonation, you can make your listeners laugh.

Do send the Fouqueray to Max Fischer with your card, and keep any other reviews for the same purpose. And send me a copy of my letter-preface. I'll have to add something when I'm back. That's all for the moment . . .

Paris, August 10, 1939

There!

I'm sending the carbon copy to Fischer.

Not a minute to write a real letter. We're leaving the day after tomorrow for Dieppe, Hôtel Métropole. Ten or fifteen days. Brittany is out of the question—Maurice has to remain in Paris, and Dieppe is only two hours away. Work on the house in Méré is coming so slowly!

Hélène Picard

Dieppe, August 21, 1939

. . . I've been here for eight days. What decided me to come was fatigue, pure and simple. La Treille Muscate has been sold, and for a pittance, thanks to Mussolini. But at least the mortgage has been paid off, and there was enough left over to buy a little house in Montfort-l'Amaury. No more South of France. Nothing doing! I say this to discourage my feeling any regrets. While waiting for the Montfort deal to be settled, I had to have some cool air, so Maurice has installed me here, in the heart of banality, with all the little bathers and elderly English ladies and "variety shows" at the ghastly casino (where I don't go, of course). But they're rather restful, providing one doesn't stay too long. Then there are two blue parakeets in the ground-floor bar who talk to me. You should hear the husband carry on when the female comes down alone to the floor of the cage. But then the silly fool goes back to him!

A ravishing storm has broken up the lovely weather. At 7:30 this morning, barefoot, I had the entire waterfront to myself. Whenever I am near the beaches we have seen together, I ask myself how I get along without you. Appropriately enough, this tail end of my letter is being written in the evening, after the storm, when the immense shaven lawns smell a little the way our old sea meadows at Rozven once did. My Hélène, I am always tenderly yours . . .

Renée Hamon

Dieppe, August 27, 1939

We are returning to Paris tomorrow morning. No one knows for how long, my little Renée. Be a good girl. If war does break out, you may be assured that Maurice will not allow me to remain in Paris. We hug you very close. But such beautiful weather! Almost as lovely as it was in 1914.

Hélène Picard

Paris, early September 1939

Bonjour, my Hélène. I'm back in Paris, naturally, since Maurice (at fifty) is not yet mobilized. We had already come back when this imbecile war became official. Maurice wants me to go away! First I'll have to know if you're there. Meantime, I come and go, and write harmless little articles. At night I lean on my darkened windowsill and wonder if perhaps you're doing the same thing, above your gardens, among your parakeets' dreams. I hug you, Hélène. I'd never have believed the human species would come to this again . . .

Renée Hamon

Paris, September 2, 1939

. . . There is no question of my budging from here. My eyes are not so good and I don't see well from a distance, so I am staying in Paris. The crew of workmen have done nothing with the Méré house, and since they are all mobilized now, it's useless to me. Even the car is requisitioned, and Maurice is waiting his turn. And your book, my poor child! Write me. If your letter catches the west wind, it just may get this far. We are both as optimistic as one can be . . .

Paris, September 15, 1939

Ma petite Renée, I had your letter, and Erna's,* this morning. It doesn't surprise me that in wartime Paris seems the only habitable place to be. The provinces are always full of cant. I found that out in 1914–18. But how to advise you about a job? Your idea of approaching Blanchard is good. He *should* find you something. Paris is already lamentable in certain parts—and grim for those who can't make their misery heard. We have just discovered that our concierge was very discreetly dying of hunger. No husband, no unemployment benefits, and . . . 800 francs a YEAR to live on. I thought it was fear that was giving her such a face. It was simply that she had nothing to eat. Now she is eating . . . Soon the people in the apartment below us are going to lack the necessities. They and ourselves are now alone in the building, and very peaceful at that. As for laughs: because of the mobilizations, Maurice is helping to edit *Marie-Claire.* Don't mention it— he's a little inhibited. What won't we see?

For the cat's fleas: use a fine-toothed comb and conduct a flea hunt every day. The cat will get used to it . . .

Madame Léopold Marchand

Paris, September 1939

Since Maurice has discovered that the suburbs and surrounding towns are just as exposed as Paris, and less well defended, he's begun to give me a little peace. This morning at eleven we remained at our window watching a passing enemy plane being fired upon. We had been waiting out 3½-hour sessions in the sub-cellar of the Hôtel Beaujolais. Magnificent sub-cellars, but they won't see me again. I suffocate from the heat, the bad air, and the odor of confined people . . . Worse, when the alert was over, we found our-

---

* Erna Redtenbacher was one of Colette's German translators and a refugee from the Nazis. Along with her lover, Christiane, she committed suicide in the face of the approaching German army.

selves locked out of our own #9, thanks to the panic of our concierge. With the help of an inventive young man, Maurice stole a ladder from the scaffolding around the Banque de France and broke the concierge's window. It made more noise than the alert.

Hélène Picard

Paris, winter 1939–1940

I'm still in town, Hélène. I certainly hoped to divide my time between here and the little Méré house, but now, for the second time in three months, it has been requisitioned for soldiers. So I stay here . . . A few bursts of antiaircraft fire have just gone off, frightening the birds. I pass through your part of town once a week, between midnight and 4 a.m., on my way to the American radio station. Sunrise this morning was so pure, with Paris deserted, not yet awakened . . . They're treating the arthritis of my hip with X-rays. And then my sessions at the dentist. "Oh, hideous age!" as my mother used to say . . .

Renée Hamon

Paris, January 1, 1940

Happy New Year, little pirate! Did your ears ring last night? We were eating your oysters, with Luc and Moune, and we talked long and well about you, and drank to your health. The oysters arrived miraculously, just before dinner. And so tidy, so clean, so moist with sea water! Pauline had her share and not one was left. Luc alone ate at least two dozen.

Charles Saglio

Paris, February 7, 1940

. . . My brother Léo (seventy-three years old) is in Bléneau, fighting without great suffering to leave this life. His heart beats only thirty-four times a minute. A strange and efficacious abyss separated him from real life and the rest of us, and now he will take with him our childhood past, and an irreplaceable cluster of memories which he has kept and classified. When he is gone, I'll no longer have anyone to consult as to what happened . . .

Madame Léopold Marchand
Nice, February 27, 1940

. . . I wish you were here. This country, this climate, this town are designed either to make you forget the war or by violent contrast to make you recall it all the more intensely. But it's enough, for me, to find that Nice is still itself, with charming weather, the sea, and flowers in bloom.

I was so exhausted when I arrived that for the first three days I only emerged from my room to eat. The rest of the time I kept to my open window and my chaise longue.

Between eleven and one in the afternoon, the crowd fills the Promenade, settling down with umbrellas, dogs, and newspapers. The nights are wonderfully calm and fresh. In other words, it's ravishing, but I'm getting impatient already, proof that I'm getting better . . .

Hélène Picard
Nice, mid-March 1940

I've been here since February 20. I finally had to give in to the doctor's advice. Overwork, arthritis, and quarrels between my red and white corpuscles! How strange it is to rest a little bit! But now it's over, just when I was getting into the habit. It's been warm, cold, sunny, stormy—in other words, Nice.

My poor old brother died suddenly eight days ago. For several weeks his heartbeat went down to 29 per minute, then 26, then 24 . . . No suffering. He never realized he was dying. I shall no longer hear him play the piano, with his chapped fingers which looked like gourds yet evoked a scintillating tone . . .

Lucie Delarue-Mardrus

Paris, March 27, 1940

. . . A year ago we sold the little house in Saint-Tropez and bought an even smaller one in Seine-et-Oise. Last week we were waiting for the paint to dry and the water pipes to thaw, and planning to move in our few shipwrecked bits of furniture, when a fragment of our fine army arrived and installed itself. I could have wept. What on earth can the army do with a three-and-a-half-room house? But there it is . . .

The dog question is difficult . . . I failed to warn you at the time that one should avoid cocker spaniels. They have frail nerves, and tend to feel persecuted—"Nobody loves me," etc. One should also avoid long-eared dogs. If a shepherd has dangling ears, have them clipped: it often reforms the character . . . I don't know why, but that's the way it is. The only occupation of a cocker is hunting, and if you don't hunt . . .

Renée Hamon

Paris, May 3, 1940

. . . As soon as I can. I still have the longest of the *Marie-Claire* pieces to do, not even begun. This evening I have the Radio-Mondial broadcast—I had simply forgotten to prepare it, the delivery boy waited an hour. Tomorrow I have to be photographed for the *Marie-Claire* issue. This afternoon I have to finish my radio talk, and there's my X-ray session at four. Otherwise, nothing . . .

Madame Léopold Marchand

Paris, June 5, 1940

. . . Tomorrow it will be a week we've lived in Méré. Maurice leaves in the morning at 8:30, works in Paris all day, and returns at 8:30 in the evening. From our charming little hill we call "the park," we've had box seats for the recent bombings. The house was fitted up in forty-eight hours and is frightful only from the outside. It will continue to be so, since no hedge trimmer is available. But the garden is charming. Not many flowers, but plenty of vegetables, beautiful old trees, and such birds! Nightingales in abundance, with their nests under our noses.

. . . My daughter is in Limousin. She was dividing her time between Curemonte and Castel-Novel, but then a lot of rich refugees, relations, and friends of Renaud's wife, with their nurses, children, and housekeepers, began to arrive, and Colette returned to Curemonte .

Paris is very warm, very calm today. The garden under my window is full of children, and why not? . . .

Léopold Marchand

Curemonte, Corrèze, end of June 1940

Since we had to leave Paris and come here where my daughter lives in the habitable part of a ruined castle, we have been in a green tomb. No news at all. Not a letter, not a newspaper, no message of any kind. It's much worse than danger. We have no idea what has become of *Paris-Soir.* We've written to Prouvost, in care of the Propaganda Ministry, but our letters don't appear to have gotten through. Where is Misz? Where are you? A century has gone by in the past fortnight . . .

Madame Léopold Marchand

Curemonte, July 12, 1940

Léo's letter has filled us with joy. Oh, if only I had stayed in Paris, as Maurice's brother and his wife have. When security means total isolation, it's nauseating, and I don't want it. This note is only to tell you that we're still in Curemonte. But I'm watching for the first chance to jump out and get back to Paris. No gasoline, little or no baggage, not even adequate linen, and then the rains . . . Léo said

Vuillard has died. Who else? We continue to know nothing . . .

Charles Saglio

Curemonte, July 1940

Cornered by the total lack of gasoline, we wait. There is no better recipe for aging. If only I'd stayed in Paris . . . But Maurice was worried about me . . . Just think, this hamlet, for the past four weeks, has had no mail, telegraph, butter, milk, automobiles, gasoline naturally, or news of any kind.

Renée Hamon

Curemonte, July 22, 1940

I should have hoped that the first letter from you would not have brought me such ghastly news. It arrived this morning, along with a letter from Christiane, full of joy and certain that Erna would soon be free. It was a letter written in June. For I am just beginning to receive mail. In this green tomb called Curemonte, we have been a *month* without letters, telegraph, telephone, gasoline, or newspapers. We could have won the war and not known it. I should not have believed such isolation was possible. We've been here since June 15. The 14th, or the 13th, the Germans arrived in Méré and we had to leave. I wanted to stay put, and in spite of everything, I'm sorry I didn't. Curemonte is a partly re- stored ruin lent to my daughter by her brother. We are famished to return to Paris as soon as it is free. Not enough gasoline yet.

My poor little one, you have endured real horrors, again. A suicide leaves us cold, if it's a question of someone we do not know. But I find myself consternated at the news that those two pure creatures chose to kill themselves. Maurice had come to feel very friendly toward Erna, especially when they were in Nice. And now you have to take care of what I call housekeeping for two dead people. How sorry I am for you!

Edouard Bourdet*

Lyons, August 31, 1940

. . . I'm so happy to know that you're in the house I remember so well, and relatively out of harm's way. And all the better if both of you liked my "ruins." I more or less passed over the isolation, which was extraordinary. I assure you, we might have been victorious and known nothing about it. My daughter is still there, but Maurice and I have come as far as Lyons. Three weeks ago, we tried and failed to cross into the Occupied Zone. At Chalon, Maurice was asked if he was a Jew, and alas, I married an honest man, and he said yes. In a few days, we'll try another entry point. We must. Having left Montfort on June 13, without being able to get into Paris, we were able to bring almost nothing with us. The money we had flows out as swiftly as the Rhone. We have more, but it's in Paris, and it isn't all that much anyway. The South of France would be fine, but we have no means of earning a living there. Luckily, *Candide* has asked me for another piece.

I won't mention Lyons. It is hospitable, but what business do I have in Lyons? . . . In this old hotel the mice flourish. There is one in particular who has been loyal to me for a month. She is very tiny, but I feed her well and she's grown so fat that she can no longer get through her mousehole. She uses the door, and while I have been writing, she has appeared twice, looking for the bits of bread I leave for her on the marble mantelpiece . . .

Hélène Picard

Paris, September 11, 1940

. . . We've arrived. It has not been easy. Where are you? Doubtless you haven't budged. I only left Paris because of family ties: my husband, my daughter . . . The devil take these loved ones.

---

* Édouard Bourdet (1887–1945), a popular playwright (*La Prisonnière*) and administrator of the Comédie Française from 1936 until his death.

If you are there, let me have a word. My arthritic hip continues to bother me, making it difficult to take the Métro, and of course we have no car. But just tell me you are in Paris, and I'll find a means to see you . . .

Lucie Saglio

Paris, mid-September 1940

. . . While in Curemonte, I finished the novella which was giving me such a hard time. Ten minutes ago, I found its title, so you'll be the first to know that it's called *La Lune de pluie*. That's the moon which has a rainbow-like halo, which presages bad weather . . .

Renée Hamon

Paris, October 26, 1940

. . . Our life is narrow and difficult these days, and constantly restricted by the hunt for nourishment. A cold wave is tormenting Paris, which has neither coal nor wood. If I hadn't bought more coal than I needed in September 1939, we'd be desperate. I'd rather die than be cold *inside* an apartment! What are people doing who have little children? Luckily, you have gas . . .

Paris, November 4, 1940

Mon petit corsaire, enclosed you'll find a check for 500 francs. With this you will get a sack of potatoes, add a chaplet of garlic and a few onions, and ship the whole thing by train, collect. Collect, because that's the faster way. And if you use a crate instead of a sack, it would be even more sure of arriving . . .

Excuse me for asking you to do this. But the battle for potatoes is truly rough here in Paris. It's unbelievable. And eggs!

Paris, November 16, 1940

. . . I'm assured that the provisions you are sending will have a hard time getting through, even in a crate. Risk one anyway. And declare its contents on the outside of the package. That is, write "apples and chestnuts." Perhaps it would be better to be even more precise and say "fruit apples."

My next book? Two novellas, quite lengthy. But it's taking so long to get them manufactured! Fayard's printer is in the provinces. And now that transport by truck is forbidden, he must resort to railroads, at a speed that deserves to be called *petite*. You'll have the book as soon as it's out, all moist as a newborn cat.

Paris, December 12, 1940

Quick, quick, a line to praise the beautiful package! I'll write presently at length, but let me just acknowledge that everything has arrived. The pink potatoes, and above all the GARLIC! Here it is absolutely not to be found. Two francs for half a clove, and even so it's not to be had. So you'll realize what a treasure trove you have sent me. And the reddish-brown onions! And the princely apples! You are a love of a little pirate—and to cap it all, the herbs!

Paris, December 25, 1940

Bon noël à mon petit corsaire! It will be a Christmas that cannot be very merry or good. What endurance we are still going to need. But you will be learning a new language, so you can assure yourself that these dark times have not been entirely barren. Here in Paris, no more woolens, nor any oranges for the past eight days. There remain a few pears at *sixteen* francs each, and beautiful apples at ten to twelve francs—always apiece. Everything else has been carried off by our "guests." I only hope they don't do the same with your precious packages . . .

I've been in bed for a week, with bronchitis and fever, though in the past twenty-four hours I've been better. But I have sworn not to go out until this cold wave is over. A great, a true and frightful cold wave is upon us, with a pure sky, and a wind in the east. Maurice tells me that Paris is completely deserted and silent everywhere . . .

Paris, January 1, 1941
Providential little pirate, alimentary little pirate—how wonderful it was to open your "treasure chest." I don't believe anything is missing, though at first I was fearful, seeing traces of the customs inspector, who behaves like a ferret in a hen coop . . . Your photograph delighted us both: that's your brave little face all right—firmly fashioned, and the cat is charming too. What luck that Gimon found you a trench-coat! I'm desolate not only at not having gone out for twelve days but at finding nothing to send you in this Paris reduced to a skeleton . . . Today, January 1, the snow has been falling for six hours and it isn't melting. The garden is magnificent, though the poor birds think otherwise . . .

As for Flammarion, I have found no trace of Max Fischer —you can guess why. So tomorrow I'll inquire at the book-keeping department, though I don't have the right to . . .

Paris, January 10, 1941
Mon petit corsaire, in order to telephone Flammarion, I have had to wait until I had a voice. For five days I haven't been able to utter a sound. This comes after a crisis of bronchitis-grippe. Now that I'm miraculously improved, thanks to injections of Dr. Jaworski's bird serum, I've been able to make a call. But one writer is not allowed to inquire as to the credit of another writer. So I contacted someone who knows you at Flammarion, someone who finds you as charming and sympathetic as can be, but whose name I wasn't able to clearly understand . . . But he'll do whatever he can, if there's any money owed you, and in any case, he'll write.

Paris, January 17, 1941
Nine below zero at my window this morning. About noon, I went out for twenty minutes—that's all I'm permitted. I

have only a dozen red corpuscles left . . . Not much to tell. Twenty-four days in retreat haven't furnished me with much news. I've begun what looks like a novel, though I don't know what to think about it, since it's moving at an unlikely pace. For once, I don't stop to arrange flowers in their vases, adjust little frames, or polish the silver . . . My daughter is somewhere in the South of France—I don't know where. At Curemonte the cold had become savage, even freezing the fruit trees. She did well to get out.

Paris, January 29, 1941

. . . Maurice now goes out every afternoon, apprenticing himself to the bookselling trade, and chiefly to out-of-print books, which have acquired a hitherto-unknown value. He goes at it with flair and passion. Perhaps we'll see him running a bookstore one day . . .

I have no idea what is going to become of the novel I've begun. On page 75, I find myself up against a stone wall. Either I must demolish the wall or make a detour.

Eggs at twenty-eight francs a dozen, you say? Here (when there are any, and there aren't), you are coldly charged three francs sixty apiece. We are using the garlic as economically as possible. The peas were very good. Send six assorted boxes of string beans; I'll send money as soon as you need it. Life here in Paris is narrow, confined, bridled. But I only rarely find myself envying friends who are in Provence. As in the other war, I want to be in Paris, melancholy as it may be.

Paris, February 23, 1941

What can I tell you, little pirate, except that I'm working? Another cold wave has chilled my desire to go out, and I've hired myself out to write . . . articles on dress fashions. Imagine! One article per month in *L'Officiel de la Couture*; one on the adaptability of the female body for *Images de France*; and one for an upcoming magazine which will be called *Le XXe Siècle*. And you know the exasperated resignation with which I work. For the time being, my unhappy novel is resting. I have no idea where it's going.

Did the great storm carry away your house? I have an extreme and melancholy longing for the ocean, for salty wind, for sea smells and warm currents. When shall I be able to breathe a tidal wind, with my arm around the shoulder of the little pirate? We must all keep a firm grip on ourselves. Tenderness is very dangerous at this time. Affectionate words and warm, tumultuous tears are just what we must refuse ourselves for the moment. But for how long?

Hélène Picard

Paris, May 29, 1941

. . . I have a neighbor who is crazy about parakeets. He is looking for a blue female to be the companion of a small blue male, and he asks if you might sell or give him one. If you have too many, he would happily take in boarders.

My Hélène, I've finished a novel. Another. It was necessary . . . Here in the Occupied Zone, it won't appear until October, but it will go off, through some hole in the hedge, to the so-called Unoccupied Zone before that. What a strange life.

Henri Mondor

Paris, May 1941

. . . I was swallowed up in a novel which I finished the day before yesterday at five in the afternoon. Provisional title: *Julie de Carneilhan*. Now you know all, except my eagerness to talk with you tenderly about your Mallarmé book. One flattering reproach (to begin): he—Mallarmé—is of a temperament almost too fragile for you. Your syntactic solidity —oh pardon!—your gift for the definitive word, your sensual and majestic charm, made me think, more than once, as I read you, of those households made up of a frail husband and a resplendent wife. Has anyone ever before called you a wife? There's always a first time! But we do miss you. When shall we dine together? Your day is our day . . .

Marguerite Moreno

Paris, June 6, 1941

But, my Marguerite, I had no idea where you were. The arrival of your interzonal card moved me deeply, even though you're far away. We've been here since September 3, leading a very narrow and prudent life. My daughter is in Curemonte. I've just finished a novel which will be serialized in *Gringoire* . . . Tenderness from the two of us.

Renée Hamon

Paris, July 8, 1941

We're suffering from the heat. Don't look for me in the *Petit Parisien* for the next six or eight weeks. I'm taking a little holiday. And imagine this: I've ordered a bicycle. It's not that my leg is that much better, but bicycling might help it.

Paris, August 15, 1941

I'm writing on whatever scraps of paper I find. There's not a single passer-by in the garden—only sun, wind, and silence this August 15. It's magnificent and I'm giving myself a work break. All this week and last I've been writing scenes for a revue at the Théâtre-Michel. I'm trying to learn a new métier, you might say, and if the revue survives, I'll have author's royalties for a month or two.

Hélène Picard

Paris, December 15, 1941

My Hélène, first let me tell you that Maurice was arrested last Friday at 6:30 a.m., the middle of the night. I won't inflict the details on you. He left very calmly for I don't know where, charged with the crime of being a Jew, of having served in the First World War as a volunteer and being awarded a medal. I'm waiting. I'm told that he may be in the barracks at Compiègne. Friends are trying to do something to help.

Meantime, I've been to see the parakeet man and left him your name, address, and the probable number of birds you have. If he still has any room in his tiny apartment, he'll let you know. One can no longer keep dogs, cats, or birds . . . My Hélène, pray to the god of poets for your Colette.

Renée Hamon

Paris, December 23, 1941

No news of Maurice other than that given me in a telephone call from another prisoner, now released: excellent morale: thirty-six men in a room; food less awful than one might think. Very good spirit of cooperation. They sleep on straw on the floor. And I'm waiting. That's the hardest part . . .

But whoever taught you to desolate a cat, to reduce him to despair, by pressing his nose in his own excrement? You not only dirty him, you poison him, literally, by clogging his nostrils and mouth! How horrible. And for the animal, what torture! Having him injected would be more merciful than a life in which you oblige him—because he cannot understand the reasons for your abominable behavior—to dread the time when he must do his business. Can his distended stomach be due to this treatment?

You're right about your book. Let it lie still for the moment. *Je t'embrasse.* I'm allowing myself to be naughty these days, to keep up my strength, but at the bottom I feel very tired. This is the twelfth day. There is *no* correspondence of any kind allowed . . .

Hélène Picard

Paris, December 23, 1941

No, *mon Hélène*, don't come to see me. It's a painful trip, and sometimes along the route they open pocketbooks and demand to see identity papers. I don't want you to be exposed to that. More important, I feel too tenderly toward you for your presence not to make me lose my grip on myself. I'm glad Guichard is taking your parakeets. I'll be able to visit them and tell you how they're getting along.

Lucie Delarue-Mardrus

Paris, January 12, 1942

Yes, it's true. Since the 12th of December, he's been a hundred kilometers away, at the Compiègne camp. They sleep on straw. Barracks. A little juice in the morning. Soup at ten o'clock. Then 250 grams of bread and a cup of *tilleul*. Impossible to write or make contact. I'm knocking at many doors. They only release prisoners who are "seriously" ill. So I wait. If only I could get a note through, or something to eat. Thank you for the lovely verses, which I keep on my table. Thank you for being concerned about my perfect companion.

Marguerite Moreno

Paris, February 13, 1942

If I haven't written, Marguerite, it was because for the past eight weeks my load has been too heavy. Maurice—"absent" since December 12—has just been returned to me. I didn't want to tell you about it—what was the point of alarming you? A huge obstinate hope persisted in me all the while, but now that it's over, I'm giving myself the luxury of being very tired.

Hélène Picard

Paris, February 19, 1942

Can you imagine me with a nightingale on my shoulder— eating and drinking and sleeping there? It belongs to a Polish lady, and came with her from Poland. He's three and a half years old, and travels about in the Métro and on buses without a cage. But he doesn't sing; "he's" a lady nightingale.

Since Maurice has been returned, I find I'm exhausted
. . . He spent eight weeks in a world where the only colors
were gray and dirty white. Now he sits in admiration before
a blue lamp against a poppy-red curtain. I've made a
tapestried upholstering for an armchair: 1840 design, with
a bouquet of dahlias under the behind, a bouquet of
morning-glories at the back, and two butterflies on each
arm. All on a tinted white background. I could have had a
career! The business of being a writer killed it off!

Renée Hamon

Paris, March 18, 1942

Neither one of us was happy to hear you suffering at the
other end of the line. The importance of affection is unbearable. Maurice will be coming to see you tomorrow. I myself
cannot use the Métro. The injections I'm having still do not
relieve the pains in my hip, and at the same time they add
muscular ache in the area of the injections.

But when will your treatments be finished? The last time
Dr. Marthe was here, she told me that she hoped it would be
soon, since the results are good.

I am going to send Fayard only a portion of your manuscript, a section which can be read independently. If I give
him the entire text, he'll want the same part *Gringoire* has
already selected and we'll have troubles. *Ma petite Renée*,
we hug you tenderly, tenderly . . .

Paris, April 22, 1942

Poor little demasted pirate, it gives me immense pain to
know how much you are suffering. I'm not good for much of
anything these days. After my X-ray sessions, I lie flat from
five until midnight. The treatments kill my appetite. Improbable as it may have seemed, I'm capable of losing
weight. But I won't give up the treatments. I'm determined
to know if my condition can be improved . . .

Paris, May 15, 1942

My stomach is burned. X-rays! The idiots! I'm applying pomade, meantime I'm red and black as far as the insides of my thighs.

Paris, May 20, 1942

. . . I have just gone to light a little candle for you at Notre-Dame-des-Victoires. The candles have become very skinny, for lack of wax . . .

Paris, June 5, 1942

My little Renée, Count Charles de Polignac was enchanted. He is going to send you half a dozen sweet little bottles of champagne, telling you that they are from *me*, but in fact they are from him. He wants to give the photographs to his son-in-law, who has lived in Tahiti a great deal. Don't forget to send him your book!

It appears that Gauguins are selling at insane prices. Watch out if you sell any of your sketches, and don't let yourself be robbed. A sketch as large as the one you showed me brings 25,000 francs. I had this from Polignac, so do pay attention. Do you have a copy of your Gauguin pamphlet? If you have, you *must* send it to Polignac, *without* any dedication, since he may want you to dedicate it to this same son-in-law, who is as charming as his father-in-law . . .

Léopold Marchand

Paris, July 31, 1942

But, my little Léo, I am the one who can best understand how you feel, that you should be unable to "show your face" at this time. But I also know that the first burning pain is not the one that hurts the most. You are at that stage of suffering at which one feels that one is going to be reasonable. Try to come visit me soon. We'll go out to the Place du Palais-Royal and sit together among the other unhappy creatures who laugh and tell each other stories . . . As for me, I'm passing through an awkward period when I forget from moment to moment that your companion is no longer with us. And I reach for the telephone thinking, "Oh I must tell Misz that . . ." I can't break the habit . . .

Renée Hamon
Paris, August 14, 1942
I was worried at having no word from you, and now your news turns out to be good. I'd give a great deal to breathe your salt air. Today I won't write at length. I'm empty and soft, because my very dear Misz, Léopold Marchand's wife, has committed suicide. For four days and four nights they tried to save her, but she had taken three bottles of pills. I feel shattered. On top of everything else, we must accept this. She was such a pure creature, so set-apart from anything ugly.

Madame Germaine Fraysse
Paris, August 19, 1942
. . . I receive good news almost every day from my "absent one." Our Saint-Tropez friends report tirelessly on their pleasure at having him there, and his perfect humor. Naturally we miss each other, but it is very different than it was last December, and I'm satisfied to know he has salt water and sunshine. I myself do not budge.

Léon Barthou
Paris, end of August 1942
Would you do me a favor? I'm entangled in a novella which takes place about 1898–1900. One of my characters is a big sugar refiner and I need to know what political and financial bigwigs of the day he would have lunch with at Larue's.

Renée Hamon
Paris, September 9, 1942
. . . the explanation for my silence is work and more work. A paper for the French Information Office is not yet begun.

I've just finished the text of a folder for the Lafayette Galleries Exposition, and completed a novella and written an article for *Comoedia*. Since I work slowly . . .

Paris, November 6, 1942

I'm guilty of neglecting my friends, little Renée. But you know I am an animal who hides herself when she feels unworthy of being seen in broad daylight. Just now I am paying with secret exhaustion for my past three consecutive years in Paris. Physically and morally I am without oxygen. That's why your old friend has been mute. Maurice writes me every day, and I write him every day. But so many days are passing and I feel so old . . .

Nothing here really deserves to be recorded—at least in my immediate vicinity. I have been working for the Free Zone, still another novella of seventy pages.* It will appear in a weekly called *Présent*, of which I've never even seen a copy. But I don't care.

As for my future publications—but keep this to yourself —my next volume will contain two long novellas and two short stories. The manuscript must conform to today's procedure, that is, a typed copy must be submitted to a committee, union, or whatever, which then decides, depending on the paper supply, whether or not to publish. After a fortnight, one of the "memberesses" of this outfit telephoned me to express her goodwill and say that she hoped to have good news for me soon. She is twenty-four years old. That's the new Europe. Nothing to say. One just waits.

Paris, December 31, 1942

. . . Did you hear me on the radio? I recorded my message under the worst conditions of grippe, hoarse voice, and anxiety about coughing. And then I forgot to listen to myself on Christmas eve . . .

* This was the celebrated *Gigi*, which had to wait until 1945 to appear in book form in France.

Paris, February 16, 1943

The laurel blossoms! What emotions a perfume can evoke, and above all, your laurels. They are at the base of our friendship. I hope you have some on your table too. On my table I have Provence as well as your Brittany, since my faithful Alice Bénard-Fleury has sent me a branch of almond blossoms. They were in bud when they arrived, but the next day they had opened. These flowers are not to be found in Paris, and I need them badly, in order to face the weather, the waiting, and my work without capsizing. For the moment I am languishing over an unbearable little job destined for a deluxe illustrated volume . . .

François Mauriac

Paris, March 12, 1943

Cher ami, I must tell you a story. Yesterday morning a prayer book was delivered to my door. It was black, ugly, and worn, just like the one I asked you to look out for. "Mauriac is certainly prompt!" I thought, but a note attached to the book explained that it came from a woman who is very ill and whom I have only known by her letters (very beautiful ones). She writes me about once a year. This evening, about 7:30, she telephoned me—which she has never done before—to tell me that she is in Paris for doubtless the last time, and will be leaving tomorrow by ambulance. I asked her why she had sent me the prayer book and she replied: "I don't know, except that four years ago I had a dream in which you appeared and asked me for it. For that particular one and no other. So when I left the hospital I sent it to you."

That's all, though Maurice and I thought the story very strange. I asked the lady if she knew you and she said no. Would you like to see the prayer book? I shall always keep it. The lady wrote on the first page: ". . . for if our heart condemns us, God is greater than our heart (John)." For more than thirty years she has been afflicted with more ills than Saint Lidwina . . .

Paris, April 9, 1943

Cher ami . . . Shortly after your visit, the beautiful story reached its denouement (though I don't believe it's finished yet). A young man close to the Princess Orbeliani brought me her last letter. He was her personal doctor and she had asked him to deliver it. When you come again, you must read it. The last sentence was interrupted by her death. She just had time to lay her pen on the bedside table so as not to stain the sheet, and she died . . . Since I have had her prayer book, I have not failed to read from it every day, as I promised you . . .

Paris, April 22, 1943

"Compromising"! Dear, dear Mauriac, that is a word which suits you as badly as it suits me. How were you even able to write it? It will be a long time before I stop reproaching you for doing so.

There are times when your plump bee slips, and fails to be equal to herself. The moment you called me was a nasty one, a time when everything looked bad, somber, hopeless, a time when I trembled for the one I love the most. I did not feel honorable. So I hid myself . . .

Excuse me for having avoided you, for avoiding you still. At the time, I swore that I'd write you the next day and explain. But before I got around to it, I caught the grippe, and when the grippe was over, I caught it again. After that I had to write *Flore et pomone* for a deluxe edition, and after that, some animal portraits (*De la patte à l'aile*) for another deluxe edition. These jobs pay for our daily bread . . .

Renée Hamon

Paris, July 8, 1943

Poor little pirate, it sickens me as much as it saddens me to hear the truth about what has been tormenting you . . . The sight of the word *elephantiasis* . . . It's as though I saw a crocodile coming out of the Tuileries pond. Elephantiasis has crossed oceans to enter your house. It's an enormity, a fantasy!

This afternoon I shall telephone Marthe. We must organize your defense. You may be sure that S———— will not leave you stranded. Maurice is horrified—how can one even imagine elephantiasis?

The weather is curious. Cold, hailstones, but no rain.

Marguerite Moreno

Paris, July 15, 1943

. . . Bresson took me by car to see his *Anges du péché*. Not bad. But Sylvie as the Mother Superior was very good. Jany Holt was good too, but then nothing is easier to play than a "bad" role. I am impatiently waiting to see you in *Carmen*. You always surprise me, making the predictable seem new. Now I'm going to bed, beneath the large warm rug of the moon. Sleep tight.

Renée Hamon

Paris, July 22, 1943

. . . I still don't have your book! Because Uckermann and I parted coldly. That "immense" contract they offered me, that "return to the cradle of my earliest success," all collapsed over a question of a few pennies. They're always the same! But I didn't give in to them and I shall not do so.

Paris, late July 1943

. . . Is it because I have not left Paris in the past four years, or because I have passed the seventy-year mark? I feel terribly old. Hurry up and get well, so you can come here and take care of me . . .

Paris, July 28, 1943

My dear little Renée, I finally have your book. Not the one which doubtless you have inscribed to me, but a copy "like everyone else," bearing your printed dedication*—a beautiful dedication, my child—I shall never have another which touches my heart more deeply. How I should love to be celebrating your appearance with a little lunch, moistened with champagne and shared with our S———! But that will come later. We'll wait for you.

Meantime, don't torment yourself about your book: it's good. It's the way it should be, and thank God it has the unevenness which is faithful to your personality. Shall I tell you that it resembles you? Yes, at the risk of making you vain, I shall. It has the taste, the color, the inimitable sound of real things. I have no more wish to see it more polished than I would wish to give you a Greek nose.

And here, just as I'm writing, comes the copy you sent me. But of course, my pirate—someday you will certainly set off again! And again become a little emblem of adventure, standing on a ship's bow with a sail behind you like a wing! The road has been hard but you'll get there . . . Wasn't yesterday the Feast of Saint Anne at Auray? You must have been thinking of her, and I was thinking of you . . .

Marguerite Moreno

Paris, July 28, 1943

Heat—the real thing. And intestinal poisoning—also the real thing. In nine days I've lost a kilo—horrors! You can hear all my folds slapping like a flag in the wind! Diet: vegetable broth and bismuth. It's not hard: the drugstore has no more bismuth and the market no more vegetables.

---

* "To Colette, whom I admire and cherish, this book born of her severe indulgence."

Maurice S———*

Paris, early August 1943

Cher ami, it's all frightfully sad. I cudgel my brains to write comforting letters. Maurice, too. But we're both overwhelmed by chagrin. I enclose the letter from Dr. Caudrelier. His last words—"In fact, nothing grave at present"—would make us all smile if it were not a question of Renée.

She tells us that she has nuns around her who are teaching her to pray. That makes good company, just as the murmur of prayers makes a good muffled sound . . .

Renée Hamon

Paris, August 7, 1943

Poor little pirate, who writes me in the middle of her own troubles! And your handwriting doesn't falter. I have studied it, and examined each letter. It remains firm and even, a sign that gives me great satisfaction. I have not yet seen S———, but this exemplary friend has written me a long, careful letter in which he speaks of your baptism and the affection the nuns feel for you. On the one hand he is unhappy at your suffering, and on the other he is full of admiration for your gaiety, your high spirits, your appetite to live and write your book about Colette . . .

Paris, September 10, 1943

Is it true that they are now letting you sit up in an armchair? And your courage is coming back? And you need pain-killing drugs less? I must have a word from you assuring me that all this is true. Because I am a Colette weakened by a morose intestine. That's why I have not written for several days. Maurice will be coming to see you. But he has been unable to do so in the last few days because he has been burdened here with all the things I cannot do. Perhaps tomorrow, or the day after, I'll see your handwriting?

* A wealthy industrialist who prefers to remain anonymous and who, along with his wife, ensured Renée Hamon's welfare during her last two years.

Paris, September 21, 1943

. . . I finally know the real nature of what I have been calling intestinal poisoning, enteritis, etc. I have a protozoa, which is to be found mostly in South America. It's called trichomonads. In our climate it proliferates only rarely. I'm the exception to the rule. What is vexing is that the little animal is virtually impregnable.

For *ten* weeks I have been really ill, and diarrhea has made it impossible for me to leave the house. I have lost weight, and above all, I have been exhausted. Now Dr. Lamy is trying to find me a specialist . . .

Marguerite Moreno

Paris, September 21, 1943

. . . Oh no, I'm not working. I'm taking advantage of the tricho. I do my tapestry and play cards with Maurice. But I cannot leave the house . . . My daughter has been here for the past week, but I've seen very little of her. Like the rest of her generation, she has "so much to do"! She's been looking for shoes, but in vain. She was offered a black-market pair for 4,500 francs. I have none myself, having gone around in sandals like a monk for eighteen years.

I've just heard about the death of Marcel Boulestin. He had been living in Paris for a year. A distraught cook who had been working for him only fifteen days found him dead in his bed this morning. He must have died as he lived, without moral or physical suffering. But I have also learned—from an Indochinese servant—that he smoked opium. He appears to have left no family.

Renée Hamon

Paris, October 14, 1943

My little Renée, I have been lax not to write you for several days. But I didn't know where to find the courage . . . All the same, you do know that I talk to you constantly, that our exchange, however mute, does not stop . . . It wearies

me to keep writing you that I am not better. This week I had
a ghastly relapse. How strange that both you and I have
attracted these tropical plagues. My little Renée, I hug you as
gently as I can. No, no, you are not a pirate, you are a very
dear little daughter—for both Maurice and myself.

Madame Maurice S———

Paris, October 20, 1943

Dear madame, thank you for having written to me. Renée's
life is a torture for her and a torment for her friends. I can
endure the sadness, but I am unable to avoid a sort of rage
when I realize that I can be of no help. The poor child so
much deserves to live. Her straightforwardness, her slightly
rough manner, have touched both you and your husband, as
they have me. And now here we are, waiting for the time
when she will no longer suffer . . .

Renée Hamon

Paris, October 23, 1943

My little Renée, my two farmer-girl friends from Morbihan,
to whom I have naturally spoken of you, have asked me to
give you a medal and a holy image. S——— will bring them
to you. I embrace you, my little pirate . . .

Maurice S———

Paris, October 30, 1943

My friend, if I write you it is not because I have any wish
to do so. It is because you are inseparable from my most
frequent, most urgent thoughts. I know perfectly well that
that poor child had to die, that it was unavoidable, even
desirable, that there was no other salvation. All the same,
now that it's over, I am deeply revolted.

I had a telephone call from Madame S——— while I was
in the bookstore downstairs. I should have called her back
but I did not. Ask her to forgive me. If I become mute and
savage when I am not happy, it is because I find my strength
in silence and unsociability.

Today it's Saturday. Perhaps you are still there, performing the task of a courageous man. When I think of her, I remember that it was here that you met this solitary little creature, who passed by without harming anyone. Her plumage was like a grebe's, incapable of soiling or becoming soiled. You took responsibility for her entirely, and tiny as she was, this was a substantial burden . . .

When we see each other again, I am sure we shall both behave very calmly. I have always taken great trouble to do so, and mostly I have succeeded. But I cannot refuse myself the sad satisfaction of telling you that I suffered. If by any chance you bring back things which you think I should have, be good enough to keep them for the time being. I do not need them, and in fact, what I do need is not to see them at this time. Now I have said what I wanted to say, and you will find my usual face when you come. I am not over it, but I am getting better.

Marguerite Moreno

Paris, October 30, 1943

. . . my little comrade-confrere-godchild Renée Hamon died last Tuesday at the clinic in Vannes. Forty-four years old, cancer of the uterus, two years of torture. She leaves two books, one on Tahiti, the other on the Marquesas Islands. A rough and proper little product of Brittany. I am going to send you her last book, which appeared a few months ago. I have only my own copy, but I'll get one from Flammarion. It's a little butch, a bit too obviously *viril*, but nothing can equal the savor of that which has been seen, and truly seen.

Paris, November 30, 1943

Dr. Marthe Lamy is going to try a new cure on me—the color violet. All intestinal parasites, it seems, die if exposed to violet. When I was a child, I was told that in churches with stained-glass windows, flies would never pass through the violet and blue rays.

Your letter was written at five in the morning. At the

same hour, I was closing my window and reading. Maurice has just given me a ten-volume series of travel books, dating from 1821, the best period. There is not a single detail which does not appeal to the purely extravagant mood, and the descriptions of South African wildlife . . . From the three-month-old sheep the size of a cow to the snake whose head is shaped like a human heart, to falling golden blocks—no, that's in Mexico—which destroy an entire village—one couldn't desire more. And when one stops to think that there is always a little bit of truth in these tales!

Paris, December 27, 1943

. . . Yesterday two young women were in raptures over your performance in *Douce*. I myself still haven't seen it. If you could see the lines in front of movie houses here . . . Until now I have hesitated on the threshold of Claudel's theater. Yesterday evening, in bed, I read Acts III and IV of *Le Soulier de satin*. As my taste has never adapted itself very easily to Claudel, I groaned as I read, exasperated by the characters and their relationships, which remind me so obstinately of Jarry. And then . . . and then, there are scenes which suspend criticism and which nearly provoke tears (the butcher's wife who goes swimming and drowns, and the last scene).

Life here in Paris is difficult. If you want to send a friend half a dozen roses, a pâté, or some fruit, you find there are no porters available. Because of his worn tires, the cyclist will not go beyond a certain arrondissement. But this is nothing. The news is that we've seen Tonton again! He found himself alone for a few hours, Robert being in the country, so he picked up a chicken, a few slices of ham, a bottle of wine, and a bottle of brandy, and turned up at our door . . .

Paris, January 25, 1944

I've sequestered myself for the past eight days, to finish a short story that had been dragging on for three months . . .

To celebrate the end of my nightmare, I attended a matinee of *Le Soulier de satin*, Vaudoyer having invited me since the dress rehearsal. Strange, but that five-hour spectacle seemed much less ponderous to me than I would have expected! Am I going to become a Claudel fan?

Paris, February 2, 1944

. . . I returned to my vomit, that is to say, I again rewrote the last page of the short story I thought I had finished. I always have the same illusions. And now *Comoedia* has asked all of us to write "ten lines on Giraudoux at once." I don't know how to write either ten lines or to do so at once. I don't even know if Giraudoux died of grippe or an attack of uremia. In any case, he spent his last night with grippe in a freezing room, and ten hours later he was dead. Cocteau tells me his dog is desperately sad.

Paris, February 3, 1944

Yes, Misia* was attacked, just in front of her own door. She was returning from the Opéra, and Christian Bérard and her frail little secretary Boulos were with her. Three or four men, who were in the same Métro car, jumped them as soon as they came up on the street. A big fellow knocked Misia down, flattened himself on her, at the same time clamping his hand over her mouth and jamming two fingers in her eyes. With his other hand he managed to wrench off her earrings.

She feared above all that she would smother. While Boulos was struggling under another man and calling for help in a barely audible voice, Bérard escaped from the third man and threw himself on the first fellow who had attacked Misia. That brave Bérard grabbed the man by the hair, and pulled, fighting like a little lion. Misia insists that she owes her life

---

* Misia Sert surrounded herself for over half a century with a court of artists and writers. She was especially provident on behalf of the Ballets Russes and Diaghilev.

to him. By that time Boulos was able to get up long enough to press the bell on Misia's front door. Automatically, the entry light came on and the door swung open. The thieves did not know it was Misia's house. They took fright and bolted, leaving the earrings on the sidewalk, where she found them the next morning. . . .

Paris, March 26, 1944

Sunday . . . My daughter has returned to Curemonte. If there were any transportation, she would visit you. This thirty-year-old child abounds in qualities which would please you. She collects homeless cats and dogs. She took with her to Curemonte a little nineteen-year-old mother with her child, whom she picked up in Paris. Surprise: it's not turned out badly! The child is six months old and superb. You can imagine how things work: "Madame, will you look after the child while I'm sweeping?" The Lord bless all this naïveté, which lives in an enormous ruin of an old château.

Paris, April 28, 1944

Our days and nights are more and more subject to air-raid alerts. It is now noon and we have had three bombardments since 4 a.m. No need to specify that the 4 a.m. one was heavy, while the ten-o'clock passed like a dream. I have sent a severe warning to my daughter, who wants to come to Paris "to do some shopping . . ."

Paris, May 1, 1944

. . . Yes, we're living in an impossible city. No more hot water, the electricity cut off for thirteen hours from morning to night. This is forbidden . . . that is illegal . . . there is a penalty for something else . . .

Paris, May 9, 1944

. . . The cold has let up a little, but at night and in the morning it's always 32 Fahrenheit. Madame Fournier took me to the Bois today, the two of us drawn by her thirty-four-year-old horse. The Bois was deserted and in full bloom, so beautiful that I could hardly bear it. I had not seen it since . . . over a year, even two years. But it's frightful to find the lakes dried up and wild iris coming up in the middle of the littlest pond.

We are still waiting. People are full of speculation. "It's set for the 16th. —But no, it's the 23rd. —On the contrary, it's the 15th of June," etc.*

Paris, June 7, 1944

It's been several days since I've written, my Marguerite. But I had to finish a manuscript which will now try to cross the border to a Swiss publisher. But . . . there are so many buts between a Swiss publisher and myself these days. And the conditions under which we work here! Yesterday, after— let's say—a sonorous night, we had seven or eight alerts. I don't budge from my armchair, but it's still not comfortable. And then since yesterday the excitement over the landing . . .

When you spoke about Missy I thought you had misunderstood the story of Misia's being attacked. But then yesterday someone phoned to tell me that indeed Missy had tried to commit suicide—something like hara-kari—a week or ten days ago. I'll try to find out just what happened, though I haven't seen her for two years. In one of those childish (she is eighty-one) turns of caprice to which she has always been prone, she *indicated* to me that she would no longer see me, and I didn't insist otherwise. Since then her memory has been slipping, and it has become more and more difficult for her to get around Paris. There was nothing gay about the end of her life . . .

Now I am going to bathe. I've been working on the end of my book since eight this morning. I've had it . . .

* D day, and the Allied invasion of Normandy, turned out to be June 6.

Paris, August 6, 1944

This morning the sky was a ceiling of airplanes. How strange it all is, and how eager I am not to die before I have seen it all!

Paris, September 8, 1944

Oh yes, my Marguerite, we have been roughly shaken up. Bombardments, cannons near and far . . . along with a touch of the comic. We had taken refuge in my antechamber, with two candles and three women from our building, one of whom was anxious to save her astrakhan coat. And Pauline said to me: "If Madame decides to go down into the shelter, Madame is surely not going to be seen in that old bathrobe!" For the proprieties are very strictly observed. But I kept my warm and battered bathrobe on and I did not go down to the shelter. Meantime, the clamor of the cannon and the shuddering of my frail old partitions cannot be described.

For the present I want to eat. I want beef stew and marinated herring, and to hell with any more tomato salads and pâtés.

During the last attack on the Place de la Concorde, Maurice was caught in the machine-gun fire and found himself trapped in the Tuileries Gardens. For three days and two nights I was in anguish, and even checked among the persons reported dead to see if he were among them. And meantime he had to stay in the garden, in a little damp ditch, and every time a human being budged, the windows of the buildings on the Rivoli fired. On the third day, there was a truce arranged by the Swedish embassy, and Maurice was able to come home, frozen, and having had nothing to eat but three green tomatoes. I admit that I received him with a volley of abuse. Without seeming to, that gentle man excels at getting into the worst scrapes—"just to see what was going on," he said.

Marguerite d'Escola*

Paris, January 29, 1945

That's frightful news about Hélène Picard. But you didn't
tell me just what she is suffering from. I thought she was in
the country, staying with her sister. Does she need anything?
I cannot visit her, my arthritis of the hip has progressively
turned me into a woman who no longer walks. But a word
from you would be immensely obliging.

Marguerite Moreno

Paris, March 1, 1945

Yes, yes, I deserve your reproaches. But I also deserve indulgence. A single word will be enough to disarm you:
work. It's turned me into a wild animal. But let's abandon
that frightful subject. What else? Well, my daughter is here.
And Morhange has been ill, after behaving idiotically;
keeping house, making meals, getting around by bicycle,
writing her music criticism (very good, too), attending con-
certs in icy halls. And then the death (ghastly) of Hélène
Picard. Like the most romantic of poets, she died in the
hospital, unknown, unrecognized, alone, and mute. A neighbor, Marguerite d'Escola, found her in an unheated ward at
Saint-Jacques, and *did not recognize her.* She spoke to her,
saw that she could still hear, and that she smiled at my name.
Madame d'Escola then left to make her husband's lunch,
promising to be back shortly. But Hélène, who had hidden
herself from everyone so that no one would ever know that
her lesions of the bone had turned her into an unrecognizable
dwarf, tricked d'Escola. When the latter returned, Hélène
had already died and her body had been removed to the
morgue. One detail, for you and for me: she died just at
the moment my *pneumatique* arrived, with its blue envelope,
still unopened, in her hand.

In the ten days that followed, I was busy with her effects.

---

* A novelist and former contributor to *Le Matin* when Colette was its
literary editor, Marguerite d'Escola was a neighbor of Hélène Picard.

For her little apartment was locked, no one had permission either to enter or to seal it, her only sister lived in Foix, and no one had the keys. When Hélène was taken to the hospital, she had for months been unable to walk except on her hands and knees. The last time Marguerite d'Escola saw her, Hélène said, "If I knew that Colette would see me as I am, I should kill myself at once!"

For ten days I have been working on a little study of Hélène's work, which the *Revue de Paris* has asked me to do. But I have never tried anything quite like this, and I'm making no progress . . .

Paris, April 25, 1945

Here, as you can imagine, we're a little agitated. The midnight radio bulletin promised a special news announcement this morning. We had it, but it contained nothing we did not know last night. My daughter has friends in Buchenwald, only one of whom has yet returned. Three or four days ago, in front of a café in the Place des Ternes, a group of women who had escaped lifted their skirts and, without a look or word, showed their legs, devoured as high as the thighs by camp dogs.

Agitated or not, I have had to work. Ferenczi has come back and naturally he wants to "put out" a book as soon as possible. With four unpublished novellas, we can manage to do so. The best of the four is called *Gigi*, and unless I'm wrong, it contains a character which will not be unworthy of Madame Marguerite Moreno if there is a film version . . . In May I'll send you the *Revue de Paris* with the Hélène Picard piece. Otherwise, we've had an April moon and glacial weather.

Paris, May 6, 1945

Far away as you are, how fast you run to bring me tender greetings. This isn't a reply, it's only a grateful kiss. You can imagine I'm a little tired out. My colleagues are unbelievably young—Rosny, 86, Descaves, 84—and they have been as sweet as possible. But Carco is very vehement toward Sacha; Billy as well. Come quickly and I'll tell you all the details.

Charles Saglio

Paris, May 6, 1945

. . . Banquet (for seven), photographers, interviews—these pleasures are not and never have been suited to my age.* Though I must admit that my gracious confreres have done their best to spare me any fuss. At the same time these past three days, what with my leg, have been, well, tiring.

Marguerite Moreno

Paris, July 17, 1945

. . . We're leaving. Two available train seats made up our minds for us. But how I wanted to see you . . .

We'll stay—though this isn't certain—for about a month. Write me at "Domaine de Mauvanne, les Salins d'Hyères, Var." The heat in Paris has gotten me down, I couldn't take any more! But if the house is too full, we'll come back. For I've set a deadline with a publisher, and these "gatherings full of fashionable people" don't facilitate my work.

Les Salins d'Hyères, August 6, 1945

Would you believe me, my Marguerite, if I told you that I'd rather be in Touzac? Of course you would. Here we are never less than sixteen at table, and all the past week we were twenty-one. Yesterday, Simone took off with a party in two cars (we stayed behind) and she brought back . . . a living sheep. The day before, it was the Prefect of Draguignan. Her decisiveness is confounding, and she feeds her guests on an astonishing scale. A grenade has just gone off

* On May 2, Colette had been unanimously elected to the Académie Goncourt.

in the garden—no one hurt. You see how extravagance takes its place in certain lives, which moreover require it as their natural element. Is it true that you are going to play *La Folle de Chaillot?* Two guests turned up at 3 a.m. with guns and hunting dogs. Simone has just bought her third automobile.

But I love the view of the salt marshes with the sea beyond. My bedroom with a terrace protects me and everyone is very kind. Yes, I'm working, and Maurice too—he's writing a play with Mirande. One of the things I love about Maurice is that nothing surprises him . . .

Les Salins d'Hyères, August 18, 1945
. . . We leave for Paris tomorrow. We've been knocking on every door for eight days, but not a seat was to be had, not on a train, a plane, or a car. Finally we'll leave tomorrow evening by way of Marseilles and a train . . . The Pasha of Marrakesh left this morning. He makes no more noise than a cat. And he dances so well! It's a pleasure to watch him dancing with the young women. There's another one who "has rhythm"!

Paris, August 28, 1945
. . . Rasimi wants to revive *Chéri.* But with whom? It will be easy enough to find a Chéri. What will be more difficult will be to find a good young leading lady of fifty. Suzy Prim claims she has just turned thirty-seven. What would you think of Marthe Régnier? She lacks presence, but she's a good actress. And she is so anxious to get back to the stage! Léo Marchand is in Vichy. I'm told that he's drinking badly.

Paris, September 4, 1945
. . . Everyone is coming back to Paris. Disorder on all sides. Simone will be back tomorrow: she has bought a fourth automobile. The Bérès—rare-book sellers—are back. Maur-

ice now has his license as a publisher and will raise the question of editing my complete works . . . Here it's been cool and stormy, but my work goes painfully. Have you picked the grapes yet?

Marguerite d'Escola

Paris, February 1946

Thank you for having taken me with you in your heart when you visited Hélène's tomb! The blue vase, the violets . . . Do you know that she accorded the color violet a strange power—satanic but not unsympathetic? Her most astonishing dreams always transpired under the aegis of an indescribable violet.

I could not possibly, by any means, have accompanied you in person. I suffer a great deal, even at night. Perhaps it's too much work. I noticed, in time, that my book of memoirs to be called *L'Étoile vesper* was at once too short and not good enough. I thought I was finished, but I've gone back to it. Three more weeks of work . . .

Marguerite Moreno

Paris, February 1946

Oh, oh, oh, oh, oh, Marguerite! What on earth can you be doing to leave me without news! Are you happy? Are you alone? A word, for a prisoner who is rewriting the end of her memoirs for the seventh time. But at least the title will please you: *L'Étoile vesper*. Meantime, a word, a phone call, good Lord!

Uriage, Isère, July 2, 1946

Just imagine—after your visit (no question of cause and effect) I began to suffer even more, so much so, so badly, that Marthe Lamy said to me: "If you delay any longer, you'll be forced to make the trip to Uriage by ambulance." But all our haste did not prevent the voyage from being a long and painful one. X-rays and injections on arrival, and

I continue to suffer day and night. But Dr. Roman—a better than average fellow—promises me relief in spite of the old-ness of the injury. What else do I want? I want to be gathering peas . . .

Uriage, end of July 1946

We leave next Saturday. I am dead tired and no wonder. Dr. Roman did not conceal from me the fact that the pain would not let up during the cure. Now I must wait two months for the results he has formally promised. We'll stop over for a week or so with friends near Grasse. The best part of it all, for me, is that I am forbidden to do any work during those two months.

Léo Larguier

Paris, September 23, 1946

I think your book of *Miscellanées* was written just for me. How could you have known that since my childhood nothing has delighted me more than eating my meals out-of-doors? During the First World War, there would be no one in the Bois, and I would bicycle out with my sardine sandwich, an apple, and a flat wickered bottle of white wine. Not much, but it was enough

. . . I've spent a dreadful summer: treatment and pain. The latter gave me no quarter . . .

Marguerite Moreno

Paris, February 1947

. . . In the name of heaven, what *is* the matter with your foot? Can it only be chilblains? If so, use an old recipe of my mother's: in a very good quality wine vinegar, marinate rose petals for a month. Then, at night, cover the chilblains with a well-soaked compress. When I was a little girl, I had no chilblains. But I used to say that I had, in order to suck the compress. I already adored vinegar.

Paris, August 7, 1947

. . . We're recovering from the heat wave. We haven't had anything so bad for well over half a century. Last Sunday, between four and seven in the afternoon, the outside thermometer went up from 36 to 40 degrees Centigrade, and I was frightened. Several times it was as high as 38 at three in the morning. The chestnut trees are burned up. The Bois is a straw mat. But in the past three days we've been able to breathe again. Yesterday morning, at dawn, it was down to 14, and I reached for my rabbit-fur coverlet.

If you happened to bend your ear toward the Palais-Royal yesterday afternoon, you would have heard Natalie Barney, Lily de Clermont-Tonnerre, and me talking about you. Those two amiable ladies had come to surprise me. For some time now, Lily has been dressing with extreme and very successful coquetry. Trying to escape the heat, we went on to Versailles, where we dined with Lady Mendel. She is ninety-one, with the thinness of a schoolgirl, and no longer lives on anything but alcohol. Dressed in white muslin, with a choker of sapphires and a silk scarf knotted into a turban to hide the absence of a wig.

All but weightless and tottering about her grounds, which are flowerless and entirely green, with hedges clipped in the British manner, in fantastic animal shapes. An evening for you, for us.

Paris, March 18, 1948

. . . Do you know what I'm writing to console myself these days? A little "Herbal" for my eminently botanical Swiss publisher Mermod, and my memoirs—for a change—in which I "talk about" Marguerite . . .*

---

* The "Herbal" was published in 1948 as *Pour un herbier*. The further volume of memoirs was *Le Fanal bleu*, published the following year, with an extensive portrait of Marguerite Moreno.

Paris, June 7, 1948

. . . The weather is thankless—"Hey, ho, the wind and the rain," as it goes in an old edition of Shakespeare which I used to read when I was eight years old . . . Otherwise, nothing new. A brief melodrama has just resolved itself. I had misplaced most of the text for my "Herbal" book. Happily, Maurice is used to this sort of earthquake, from which he has rescued me before. But while it was in progress I lost my head.

The local strawberries are tasteless this year. I'm sure yours are better. Marthe Lamy (one of my two doctors) keeps a mouse in her room. She found that it was keeping her awake as it would come and go through a hole in the woodwork. So she plugged up the hole, locking the mouse in her room, where she feeds it . . .

Hyères, July 8, 1948

My Marguerite, your dictated letter has arrived, but you tell me too little about what's happening to you. I beg Pierre to enlighten me. I'm uneasy already, telepathically. We've been here forty-eight hours and I suffer in the usual degree. Everyone is very nice, but I tell you this only so you won't worry about me and concentrate on your own illness. But *what* illness?

Pierre Moreno

Hyères, July 15, 1948

Pierre, my dear friend, I have just tried to send you a telegram. Pierre, it's very hard. With the egoism of a great affection, I allow myself to say, "we do not deserve this." And when I say "we," I am asking you to let me be a member of your family. I did not see Marguerite leave, I was unaware of her leaving. And how sad it is! She was so little made for dying . . .

Hyères, July 16, 1948

Dear Pierre, you know that I have been thinking of you and of Marguerite during these hours in which you have been accompanying her to her grave. Later you will tell me what I could not bear to hear at present. It is lucky for me that I am here, among people before whom I cannot let myself go. It is lucky, too, that my arthritis pains are sharp today —they distract me . . .

Hyères, July 25, 1948

Dear Pierre, I think of her and I think of you. I read the newspaper articles which speak of her, and when my turn comes to recall the stages of our friendship, I hope to speak worthily of her . . .

Jean Cocteau

Grasse, late July 1948

Dear Jean, how right you were to write me. To you I can say the truth—that I don't know when I shall get used to her dying. Fifty-four years of friendship! And not an easy or unbroken friendship, by any means! A friendship which was threatened, which might have perished, but which survived everything . . .

Pierre Moreno

Paris, January 8, 1948

. . . Marguerite's book* seems to be having a success. I spend my time stumbling against her absence, and it hurts. But I prefer that hurt to indifference . . .

Paris, April 13, 1949

I've been very ill, and I've never thought so much about Marguerite. During my bad nights and coughing fits, I cling to her memory and image. What bitterness and sweetness

---

* A volume of memoirs and theater portraits, *Souvenirs de ma vie*, with a preface by Colette.

are combined in a fidelity as involuntary as ours! I have missed Hélène Picard and her richly provincial genius, but in all the losses I've known, nothing can compare with the shock I feel every time I remember Marguerite . . .

Paris, December 29, 1949

The epistolary part of my "festivities" this year will be cursory. Why? Because my friends are not very numerous any more. And because my work seems a little sour to me. And then, these "festivities" only recall the absentees—and in particular, Pierre, our Marguerite . . .

My wits are lacking today. Is this because I'll be seventy-seven in thirty-one days? Or because I have just been arranging in what I call my cemetery of affections the little pen drawing of Marguerite's tombstone? A little of both . . .

Monte Carlo, March 8, 1952

. . . Yesterday I was talking at length about Marguerite. Happily, the remembrance of what I have loved best remains intact . . .